Finding Your Perfect Soulmate or Business Partner

Learn More About Yourself and Others Through the Science of Numbers

By
David E. Smith Jr.
with
Bernard Adolphus

DESTECH PUBLISHING DESTECH NEW YORK

Destech Publishing, Inc., Peekskill, NY 10566

©1998 by Destech Press Publishing

2nd Printing

All rights reserved. Published 1997

Printed in the United States of America

Library of Congress Cataloging in Publication Data

ISBN 1- 8 91641-00-X

Cover design by Greg Duncan

Book design and cover enhancement by Tina Malonis

ATTENTION COLLEGES AND UNIVERSITIES, CORPORATIONS,
AND PROFESSIONAL ORGANIZATIONS: Quantity discounts are
available on bulk purchases of this book for educational training
purposes, fundraising, or gift giving. Special books, booklets, or book
excerpts can also be created to fit your specific needs. For information contact: DESTECH Press, Marketing Department, 13 South
Division Street, Peekskill, NY 10566.

HOW TO CONTACT THE AUTHORS

David E. Smith Jr. and Bernard A. Adolphus provide consulting services for selected authors, businesses, associations and nonprofit organizations nationally and internationally. Requests for information about these services, as well as inquiries about their availability for speeches, workshops and seminars should be directed to them at the address below. Readers of this book are also encouraged to contact the authors with comments and ideas for future editions:

Destech Press Publishing Inc.

Inquiry Department

13 South Division Street

Peekskill, NY 10566

ph: 914-739-8053   fax:914-739-8007

email: perfectsoulmate@hotmail.com or

destech@pcrealm.net

website: www.destechpress.com

ACKNOWLEDGEMENTS

We would like to express special gratitude to those that made this book become a reality. Thanks to the countless people who are too numerous to mention for their financial support, or supportive friendship.

DEDICATION

To the Creator, My Parents and Grandparents

CONTENTS

PREFACE

Welcome to the second edition. This book has been designed to make reaching and calculating birth dates much easier to understand with more thorough explanations. Here, you will be able to navigate through chapters faster and learn important information about any person the reader may be intrigued with.

As to the creation of this book, it was a fascinating experience; especially when you are familiar with this science. Although like life, full of checks and balances, it had many difficult aspects to contend with. Call this the preface, introduction, foreword or whatever; that is all publisher talk. It really doesn't matter. The bottom line is, that this book was written in order to communicate to the world. Communicate the fact that, there are many gifts placed on this earth made for people that we as a whole are overlooking. Positive gifts and talents that can actually help make our lives much easier to live.

This book was created and compiled to introduce you to a science handed down by the Universal Creator to the ancient Egyptians. This science, like others, crosses all barriers, no matter what race, color, creed, walk of life, life experiences, gender, religion or degree of education involved in your life. This is a book that can help all mankind.

I say this first, to dismiss the likelihood of some of you that may be devising an early and unwarranted opinion that this science may somehow impede in what you already believe in. Mainly those of you that are very religious, and therefore conclude you can't read this book because of God, Allah, Jehovah or that the Bible says "whatever".

Readers must be open- minded to accept the fact that the science of numerology, (the study of numbers), is an actual science used since the beginning of time. If it wasn't, we as the human race would not be able to: measure objects, tell time, or have an ordered universal system. In other words, everything you do in this world amounts to numbers if you really sit down to think about it. Whether you use money to buy something; use your social security number for employment; locate a street address; telephone number or whatever; it all falls back to numbers.

Here in my book, numbers can be used to help improve your life and help you develop a better understanding of yourself. Numbers can also help you to understand others that you are, or might become involved with in the future. It is a positive science, and leads you to building better and healthier relationships. Furthermore, I have placed it in an easy to read and calculate format that will take only minutes to comprehend. Once you have learned how to calculate birth dates of people, then you can learn about anyone, anywhere, at any time.

Since this science works so well for people, many questions have come my way, and many more are sure to come. I would like to share one of them with you. Whether I am conducting a speaking engagement, seminar or workshop, people ask do I have a perfect soulmate? If not, how am I qualified to write a book on such a topic? Well, my answer now is and in the future will be, this is not a book of my personal fulfillments, and I offer no opinions in the book at all. None! The only thing expressed in this book, is information derived from the actual science of numerology.

Therefore, people can read it without bias, or consulting with anyone but themselves on any relationship they may happen to encounter. The true question that should be raised is, how are the people that use this book going to make a positive change within themselves, in order to build the healthy relationship they seek? This is a legitimate question, since the reader is provided with general characteristics they can work with. This is surely a question that can be turned back to the person(s) who may ask such a question; for once they are able to understand themselves, then the answer will become clear.

I decided to self-publish this book in order to make sure that this work and research I compiled is not wasted by sitting on the back burner of a huge publishing conglomerate collecting dust. I want to get the word out as soon as possible, so that we can all have prosperous relationships without being subjected to restraints or negative opinions of a big publishing house. If a big publishing house were to handle the release of any of my books, my books would end up in the sole control of the direction of publicizing the book. In other words, they would have the power to determine if and when society needs such a book to read, excluding the author of any discretion.

A large publishing house can basically tell an author, that they will decide to never release it and drive a determined hard working writer insane. This is why I was careful not to give up my exclusive rights. A monetary advance and a back room full of undistributed books would not make me happy, or be fair to you, the people. You, the readers, are of utmost importance to me.

People successful in the art of love consider themselves to have the knack of being in the right place at the right time. How many people can actually depend upon that knack? The analysis that numerology uses reduces the dependency on luck to determine suitable spouses, companions, business partners or lovers. These analysis can provide you with the opportunity to seek without doubt, the soulmate or business partner that may be right for you.

Yes, it is true that there is a right time and right place for romance, and more importantly, there is a right person for you to be with. However, if you know the person who is compatible with your own personal number(s), then you have a head start on the road to success in love or business matters. You will find out which months of the year and which days of the month your ideal soulmate would be born on. Likewise, you will also find out which birth months and dates make for unsuitable lovers or spouses. Many people complain after marrying, that if they only had some kind of "crystal ball" to see the future. Then, an awful lot of pain and heartache could have been avoided in choosing an incompatible soulmate.

This book is for everyone. Although, people who are very young, teenagers, and adults in their early twenties, may find some things a little hard to relate to. The reason for this is, that they still have a lot more maturing experiences to go through before a majority of characteristics and attributes fully develop. If a reader falls into one of the above categories, these readers need.

Finally, I would just like to say that I would gladly enjoy hearing about your experiences; confidentiality kept of course. Tell me how you handled a particular situation(s), and how you improved your relationships.

David E. Smith Jr.

INTRODUCTION:

Numbers in General

Our complex universe is actually made up of nine single digit numbers: 1,2,3,4,5,6,7,8 and 9. (The number zero represents a cipher and is not used when calculating birth dates.) This is a scientific fact. However, those that are skeptical or believe otherwise, are justified to question this until they see proof. Lets do a little breakdown. Take any number (or as mathematicians would say, "positive integer"), add the digits and reduce them to a single digit. The total will be a number from 1 to 9.

For example:

Take the number 383. Simply add 3+8+3, which equals 14. It is not a single digit yet, so we must proceed. Now add 1+4 which equals the single digit 5. There you have it, a number from 1 to 9.

Lets try one more example, and if you still don't believe, you may continue to take any whole numbers you wish and determine for yourself. Take the number 7417. Add 7+4+1+7=19. Add 1+9 which equals 10. 1+0=1. The number 1 is the single digit. Now that you understand, it is time to move on.

Number Symbolism: The Meaning of Each Number

Each of the nine numbers has its own symbolism and unique qualities. If a particular number belongs to you personally, then so do the qualities of that number. Qualities that can help you determine simple or complex questions such as: are you going to gain and keep a business or loving relationship? Will you have a peaceful and happy home? Will you do well in business ventures or in a corporate environment?

You may want to know whether or not you or another person is destined to be a leader or a follower; rich or poor; popular or unpopular; spiritual or worldly? Much of this type of information has already been pre-determined by your personal number(s). Knowing what you can expect of yourself is winning half the battle. The other half is knowing what to expect of others. Correctly relating to people, and handling them with understanding in different situations, can lead you to a more prosperous livelihood.

Hopefully, as you read on, you may realize that you no longer need to take relationships for granted, hoping for things to work out. You can actually be prepared to make the right decisions. Knowing your personal number(s) and the numbers of others will surely help you better understand your own nature and the nature of others.

Number Attributes: The Aspects that Correspond with the Symbolic Number.

This book discusses both the negative and positive sides of personal attributes which are all based on what each individual's particular number(s). It also explains how to cope with personal numbers that cannot be changed. It also gives you the incentive to take charge of those personal attributes that are unpleasant or may need improvement. In other words, this book is designed to help you know what kind of social situations to avoid, and on which occasions you or others will be at their best.

How many times have you wished to be able to predict the future? Since that is not totally possible, the next best thing is to be as fully prepared for the future as possible.

- Recognizing those people who are truly your friends,

- Understanding those who would be the most compatible lovers

- Realizing when more spirituality is needed, or

- Determining what the best career choice would be for you...

All these things, and more, can be answered in this book as we unlock the secrets of your personal numbers.

Numbers and their Representations:

Each number between 1 and 9 is represented by a different set of characteristics. Zero is an enhancement integer.

The following list outlines each number's characteristics. The meaning of each of these numbers is explained more thoroughly in its own chapter.

#1 : Independence and Confidence

2 : Cooperation

3 : Expression and Sensitivity

4 : Practicality and Stability

5 : Freedom and Discipline

6 : Balance, Responsibility, Vision and Love

7 : Trust and Openness

8 : Abundance and Power

9 : Integrity and Wisdom (The Humanitarian that represents all numbers)

0 : Enhances special talents

Material Possessions and their Vibrations

In addition to numbers, there are also colors, gems, crystals, planets and days of the week that represent the most positive vibrations. These vibrations work in conjunction with their associated numbers.

For example: Lets use the number 30.
If you arrive at 30, you will see (30/3).
This comes from the destiny adding up to 30. Then 3+0. Therefore 30/3.
3: Expression and Sensitivity
0: Enhancing Special Talents (The number "0" adds extra emphasis to the main number, which here happens to be the number 3.)
The number 30/3 is also associated with the following material possessions and vibrations:

Color: *Yellow*

Gem: *Topaz*

Crystal: *Galena*

Planet: *Venus*

Day of the Week: *Wednesday*

The best day to do a project or have a job

interview is the third day of the week, Wednesday. You should wear some yellow on that day. Venus is your planet. As for jewelry, wear the gemstone, topaz and the crystal Galena. This is not to say that you cannot wear anything else, or perform a project or job interview on another day; it means that the vibrations your numbers carry work best with all of the combinations above.

Determining Characteristics of a Person

There are Two Ways to Determine the Characteristics of a Person, by birth date or destiny number.

OPTION #1:

Determining Characteristics through the Birth Date (also known as birth path).

First things first—many people do not wish to give their age. In this case you can calculate the Birth Date or Birth Path with the day of the month the person was born on. Then proceed by doing the following:

Example 1

The birthday is June 23rd

Take the date of birth, the 23rd, and add the two digits together to arrive at a single digit. In this case: 2+3=5.

This person is a 5 in numerology.

Go to the chapter of the number 5

(The Freedom Group)

Example 2   The birthday is March 7th

Take the date of birth, the 7th, and

use it as a single digit.

This person is a 7 in numerology.

Go to the chapter for the number 7

(The Group of Trust and Openness).

Example 3   The birthday is April 29

CAREFUL! CAUTION! WARNING!

Observe this number, it is a MASTER NUMBER Please do not overlook this example. Any number when reduced to a repeating double digit, or in other words has two of the same numbers before reducing it, is a master number and is not to be reduced right away. Take the date of birth, the 29th, and add the two digits together.

In this case: 2+9=11.

Do not reduce this number any further to get a single digit. This is a repeating double digit. This person is a Master 11 person in numerology. Go to the chapter of master numbers. You will be instructed as to when it can be reduced to a single digit.

Note: If in reading about a master number, such as the 11, and it doesn't seem to fit as well as it should, this is probably because that person has not yet harnessed its powerful energy. That person then reverts to the number two (1+1=2) instead. Turn to the chapter that discusses the Cooperative Group. Read both the Master number and the Cooperative Group to determine which attributes most apply.

Now try these dates before you go on:

August 25

Single Digit: _____

Chapter: _____

October 22

Single Digit: _____

Chapter: _____

December 1

Single Digit: _____

Chapter: _____

ANSWERS

August 25

Single Digit: 7   (Use the 25 to get 2+5=7)

Chapter: This is a seven person. Go to the chapter for the seven person. (Trust and Openness)

October 22

Single Digit: 4 or Master 22

(Use the 22 and do not reduce, unless energy doesn't seem to be harnessed yet, then revert to 2+2=4).

Chapter: This is a four person. (Practicality and Stability). Go to the Master 22 chapter and the chapter concerning the number Four Person.

December 1

Single Digit: 1

Chapter: This is a one person. Go to the chapter that represents the One Person. (Independence and Confidence)

OPTION #2:

Finding the Destiny Number

This is done by adding the Month, Date, and Year of birth.

Example 1

August 25, 1962 = 8/25/1962

8+2+5+1+9+6+2=33

Use the 33 to get 3+3=6

Master Number 33/6

Leave the number at 33/6

Notice how we use two sets of digits, the 33 and the 6.

Look up the 33/6 which is already provided for you under the master number section. Then, look up the number six for the general understanding. Remember, not everyone has or even knows how to harness such a special energy; if they possess a master number.

Example 2

May 19, 1963 = 5/19/1963

5+1+9+1+9+6+3=34

3+4=7

34/7

This is a number 7 person in numerology, derived from the 34. Look up the specific number 34/7 listed in the book in Chapter 7. Go to the chapter for the number 7 person (The Group of Trust and Openness), and then find the 34/7. Remember to read both sections for a more comprehensive understanding.

Lets try these examples:

January 29, 1965

February 17, 1922

July 4, 1936

September 14, 1956

ANSWERS:

January 29, 1965 = 1/29/1965

1+2+9+1+9+6+5=33/6

Here is Master Number 33.

Look up both numbers 33/6 and the number 6.

The 33/6 considered to be more powerful than the six alone. 33/6 encompasses all energies.

February 17, 1922 = 2/17/1922

2+1+7+1+9+2+2=24/6

Look up a 24/6 person and the number 6.

July 4, 1936 = 7/4/1936

7+4+1+9+3+6=30/3

Look up 30/3 and the number 3.

September 14, 1956 = 9/14/56

9+1+4+1+9+5+6=35/8

Look up 35/8 and the number 8.

Summary, Overview, and Understanding the Makeup of Each Chapter

Everyone has an association of two numbers. Both the birth path and the destiny number apply. The birth path has characteristics in its own right, and are relevant. However, they are not as controlling as the single or Master destiny numbers of the person. The destiny number carries much more weight than the birth path. Therefore, you can read both the characteristics or traits of a person whose birth date adds up to the number two, and you can read characteristics or traits of that same person whose destiny numbers may be a six. Just remember the destiny will have much stronger influence than the also relevant birth date. Both numbers play a role, and can be compared to each other.

In summary, the most significant number is the single digit destiny number. Also important are the general characteristics of each single number. This destiny number combination will contain the most significant and detailed information of a specific person.

EXAMPLE:

The Number 2 Represents the Cooperative Group
The Destiny Number 20 is the number 2 enhanced.

The destiny number is the life path derived by finding the total sum of the month, day and year of birth and then reducing it to a single digit or master number. This is the number that contains lessons to be learned in this person's lifetime.

2: Cooperation and Relation
0: Inner Gifts

Twenty (20) is the double digit derived, and 2 and 0 are each digit's representation before they are reduced to a single digit 2. These double digits have a major influence in the destiny number which is a part of its make-up. These double digits are important both when reduced to a single digit and when remaining as a Master Number.

The combination 20/2 is associated with the following material possessions and vibrations:

Color: *Orange*

Gem: *Moonstone*

Crystal: *Rutile*

Planet: *Moon*

Day of the Week: *Monday*

The Birth date or Birth path :

The Birth path or Birth date is derived from the total sum of the birth date 1/20/68, (the 20th) reduced to a single digit or Master Number.

NUMBER 2: Compatible Soulmate,

Business Partner, Spouses and Lovers.

Persons born on the 2nd, 11th, 20th or 29th, of any given month, or a destiny number that adds up to a number 2, is a two person, (For example, someone born on October 20th: 2 + 0 = 2). Communicates devotion from the emotional part of their nature.

1

The
Independence
Group

Compatible Soulmate, Business Partner, Spouse and Lover

A person born on the 1st, 10th, 19th or 28th of any given month, or with a destiny number that adds up to a number one, is a number one person. (For example, note someone born on April 10th: 1 + 0 = 1). The number one person tends to think from the mind and not form the heart.

Color: *Red*

Gem: *Ruby*

Crystal: *Garnet & Pyrite*

Planet: *The Sun*

Day of the Week: *Sunday*

Traits

The one person communicates love and emotion from the intellectual side of their nature, foremost by reacting to situations using their brain power rather than their heart. In encountering this type of person, you will find that they want to dominate and be the leader in most, if not all, situations -- especially if there is no threat to their well being. Basically, they love doing things by themselves. It is an uncontrollable urge.

Since their personality is ruled by a strong desire to be free from influence, fulfilling all that they set out to do is a priority. Such determination usually brings achievement. The one person will not wait for others to have the idea, but usually initiate the thoughts themselves, and see them through until completion. No need to offer help, unless they ask, for they'd rather work alone. They prefer to be a loner, and they seek praise and opportunities in order to create great things. Such individuals are for themselves, and believe that it is best that way in order to help others.

They are usually capable of doing large or great things, naturally, since their independence makes them think on a larger scale. It is their independent nature that keeps them interested in the large, overall plan, as opposed to details in any project. They are not particularly interested in minor details. When they are working on their own, they feel that the world, money, success, and fame at their fingertips. If they use their internal power wisely, the one energy bursts forth freely, with positive, dynamic energy, power, and they can become luminous with life. They possess the most magical way of minimizing problems and getting to the heart of matters. When setting their mind to focus on what they want, they usually get it in record time!

If involved in a relationship with the one person, expect them to be the explorer, the trailblazer and trend setter in most that they wish to do. When they set the pace, others follow, and usually its never the other way around. Whether they are encouraged or realize for themselves, they are at their best when considering striking out on their own. New frontiers do not frighten them. No new challenge intimidates them. They tend to base opinions on their experiences, and eventually direct others who value their advice, down the correct path.

On the negative side, the one personality, when angered, can display temper tantrums, stubbornness, idleness, pessimism and emotional outbursts. Be careful, you can misinterpret the number one person to be egotistical and self-centered. It is not too far from the truth since they always look out for " number one". Remember, this is the number of superior brain power, courage and energy but "practice" is a weak point for them. It is highly probable that they are impatient and/or boastful. Many of them need to let people know that they exist in the world.

It is the lack of patience that can put them out of control. When impatient, the number one can be restless, irritable and irrational, blocking all positive energies necessary to achieve what they initially set out to do. Without thinking, they can be sharp with the tongue, insensitive and scathing to anyone who gets in their way. Others may feel hurt or stepped on.

The number one person will be a choice lover, mate, business partner or friend so long as they can be "captain of the ship" in their relationship. The number one individual is imaginative, innovative, resourceful and rarely accepts changes in their opinions. The number one wishes never to abide being second in any phase of their life.

A special note: Anyone born on the 19th of the month, for reasons not explained in this book, are usually unmarried, or divorced; and if married or in partnership, are very difficult people to live with. The relationship can end quite abruptly without them ever looking back. However, if their positive spiritual nature takes hold, they will also make an effort to stay friends with a significant other.

Career

It can be expected that the one person will be comfortable in making a thriving career in administration or management. Occupational fields such as aviation, invention and science, engineering, education, politics, or entrepreneurship would make them shine. These people would make great senators, congressmen or presidents. History points to several dictators and authoritarians who were classic examples of the number one personality. Their directness and candidness in their dealings with others is legendary. The number one reacts well to resolution and reason, making them very good in the leadership role of an organization.

Compatibility

Their sense of security in communicating is mental. It is part of the number one's personality to respond from a position of determination, logic and reason. This number is assigned to the planet of the Sun, and the number one will find their most compatible relationships are with those born in the months of February, April, and August; as well as with those born on dates adding up to the numbers 2, 4 or 7.

Persons born in the months of January, May and October may be at the root of antagonism and dilemmas for the number one person. Also, those born on dates adding up to the numbers 6 and 8 can cause adversity and misfortune for the number one. The first day of the week, Sunday, is their best day

19/10/1

1: Independence and Confidence

9: Integrity and Wisdom

0: Amplified Gifts and Resources

Color: *Red*

Gem: *Ruby*

Crystal: *Garnet & Pyrite*

Planet: The Sun

Day of the Week: Sunday

Say hello to a marvelous and creative person with a magnetic and most charming personality. A personality which makes it easy for others to be attracted to them. When working among others, others feel that they are in good company and receive respectful advice from these proficient speakers. Whenever they want to communicate something in particular for the good of others, they are looked upon as strong leaders and teachers that give guidance in what they do by example. Even though independent and confident, they shine brightest when working in areas of service to others, no matter what the task or occupation. They can display a great and genuine interest in others, and are usually quite social.

When in sync with themselves, they can feel the higher laws of a spiritual nature, not even knowing exactly what it is that is making them feel that way. Whatever, they do know it feels great to them. They are sensitive in nature, and their special talents bring about a higher sense of wisdom and integrity that gives them a great reasoning ability.

On the other hand, whenever energy is withheld, meaning their positive energy, expect this person to lash out with anger due to frustration and display a very short temper. Such anger is not because it is innate within themselves or because it is others always making them feel that way, but it is because they are mostly angry at themselves.

Insecurity begins to set in and they become stubborn, confused and out of sync with their inner-selves. Instead of working their independent nature, dependency may become an ugly creature in their lives. So much so, that they may find themselves becoming indulgent or moreover, overly indulgent in liquor, drugs and tobacco. In other words they are prone to addiction if they are not careful.

In relationships, they can be very romantic and their touch can be a feeling of the most sensual and healing. All of their charm, charisma and good spirit can make people feel wonderful, as if they were touched by some sort of a mystic healer. As far as having a long term relationship, they find it very difficult to be intimate for a long period of time, therefore a person involved with them should not always expect it to last for long.

The slightest thing that the 19/10/1 person sees as negative in a person they are involved with can lead to a total turn of the tides in the relationship. Basically a relationship can turn from good to ugly. Quickly! Head strong, bitter, bossy, frustration becomes expressive in their actions, and by nature, they rarely ever have a problem expressing themselves. Remember, their thoughts come directly from the mind and not the heart. Some days they can feel from the heart, and other days they revert back to what they think works best for them, which are thoughts from the mind.

It cannot be emphasized enough that most of 19/10/1 persons [reasons not explained in this book] are unmarried, or divorced; and if married or in partnership, are difficult people to live with. The relationship can end quite abruptly without them ever looking back. However, if their positive spiritual nature takes hold they will also make an effort to stay friends with a significant other.

28/10/1

2: Cooperation and Balance

8: Abundance and Power

1: Independence and Confidence

0: Amplified Gifts and Resources

Color: *Red*

Gem: *Ruby*

Crystal: *Garnet & Pyrite*

Planet: *The Sun*

Day of the Week: *Sunday*

Independent in nature, 28/10/1 individuals have a creative and confident way that helps them to be more cooperative in working with other people. When in tune with themselves and they come to recognize their authoritative abilities, they will find most of their success comes from balancing their independence and cooperation with others. When their working energy is very high, they feel as though they can tackle anything that comes before them, with or without help.

In issues of money, they tend to do well in the handling of it; once they get it. They are usually effective in authoritative positions, or when they function in an executive capacity, with great administrative skills in a corporate environment. This is particularly true in the workplace. In relationships they tend to be in control and make success a daily event, which satisfies them greatly.

The 29/10/1 is sensitive and sincere to the feelings of others. They can be oversensitive when it comes to criticism of themselves from others, whereby they will usually take things to heart and dwell on what was said to them. This is not to say that they are like this all the time, but more so than other people who have numbers adding up to the number one energy. Their emotional energy makes them feel very vulnerable and easily hurt. This energy is quite strong and expressive.

If their mind is cluttered with too much negative energy, they will find themselves feeling insecure or lonely, somewhat overly sensitive, inferior to those that have authority over them and dependent. Anger, frustration and nervous tension will tend to aggravate them possibly causing severe health problems.

In relationships, they tend to be more

quiet, shy, conservative or reserved, than the next person, but that is because they have a difficult time in expressing themselves emotionally. They may be too busy trying to mentally cope with all the activities that are going on around them.

The 28/10/1 individual possesses a sense of security that keeps them in control of any situation, and with their positive working energy, they do not try to be in total control of their relationship. To be bossy and manipulative is not in their best interest, but can become a role in their relationship. They tend to have a good sense at judging character of others, no matter who they tend to work with, making it somewhat easier for them to eventually adjust to a relationship.

37/10/1

3: Expression and Sensitivity

7: Trust and Openness

1: Independence and Confidence

0: Amplified Gifts and Resources

Color: Red

Gem: Ruby

Crystal: Garnet & Pyrite

Planet: The Sun

Day of the Week: Sunday

The typical nature of the 37/10/1 individual is very social, warm and friendly. Whether at a party, or business function they are great conversationalists. They have a way with words that keep them noticed, and possess a charm and charisma to be admired. They are creative and inspiring, with a spiritual fervor about themselves that make people truly notice them.

37/10/1 individuals usually find themselves analyzing what is said amongst them. They make their own convictions as to what is meant by the statements of others, without agreeing with the convictions of others. Even though they may like to find out information about others and/or report information about others, they are pretty much self centered. They can be extremely quiet and shy unless they get to know you. So quiet at times, it may even hinder them from getting a job or finding a soulmate;

all because during an interview or social gathering, both requiring personal expression. This is not new to them, and they are very aware of this reserved nature. Once they overcome this expression issue, they will discover many of the beauties life has to offer them.

They are not easy people to understand, and many times they are busy searching to find out more about themselves. The 37/10/1 person does not portray any easy perceptions. The 37/10/1 person finds it difficult to be open with people as well as trust in them. Their conservative nature portrays that they do not request anyone to trust them either. Set in their own ways in thinking and acting, it can be said that they are not the most conforming or adapting people in the world. 37/10/1 people tend to analyze anything and everything, all for the purpose of understanding. Many times without letting others know that they are actually searching.

There is no question about it, these individuals unequivocally enjoy, and have no problem with, being different from others. Why is this so? Well, they tend to operate on a different level mentally. They usually take an alternative approach when it comes to taking on a task or long term project; usually reaching the correct solution to any given problem. When working on a project or reaching a solution, expect them to take an independent and creative approach that usually satisfies themselves and others who are judging their work. The 37/10/1 can work almost like a scientist with an inventor's mind and a mechanical type of approach.

Difficult to get to know, and unless they really look to invite you into their world, you would believe that they are outright aloof or cold. Fear not, it is just a facade, so expect their world of welcome difficult to penetrate. They often reveal little about themselves unless other energies and circumstances change.

When relaxed, and they feel they have gotten over many issues about you, which they created in their own mind, they are positively outgoing individuals. Creative and independent, you can leave it up to them when it comes to activities. Rest assured, they will always have a good idea.

In the negative, call them dependent, angry, frustrated or even cold. This coolness is not so much directed at any particular person or group, it usually stems from what they are fighting within themselves. Lack of a spiritual understanding and listening to their own heart is more of an issue in their lives than anything else. They would not experience such issues to begin with if they did not depend on their own mental faculties as much. Alcohol, tobacco and drugs may easily become a part of their lives, not so much socially, but in the form of addiction.

If working a relationship from the negative side, expect explosive anger and frustration from the 37/10/1 individual. They will definitely remember the past and tend to bring it up, in your face, time and time again. Many times they will mention things that bothered them but kept to themselves for analyzation. They can even give you a detailed account of what occurred, what they thought, and what you said, occasionally. They may become dependent and place more pressure on the relationship than necessary.

Definitely expect them to bring up the topic of trust and openness in a relationship. Letting them know that your heart is in the relationship makes them feel more at ease when becoming open with you about themselves, and about anything involving the relationship. Remember, they can be so self centered at times, that their mind rules their thinking. They are dependent upon that mental thought so highly, that what they consider to be issues in their lives are apt to play tricks in their head -- more so, because they are always busy analyzing situations in their relationship. Some situations, if not many, are immaterial and they usually come to this conclusion when it is too late.

Since they tend to always seek an understanding of things, they tend to be on the quiet side, however not exactly the shy side of expressing themselves. This is until they really believe they have gotten to know you well and are able to handle situations involving a significant other. Remember they are usually busy in the mental thinking about things that could affect them and the relationship; giving rise to their own world. This definitely helps give them the appearance of being good listeners, and in fact they are.

46/10/1

4: Stability and Process

6: Balance, Responsibility, Vision and Love

1: Independence and Confidence

0: Amplified Gifts and Resources

Color: Red

Gem: Ruby

Crystal: Garnet & Pyrite

Planet: The Sun

Day of the Week: Sunday

Meet the independent, but practical individuals. They are more capable of balancing situations in work and relationships than their one counterparts. When placed in a dilemma or situation that calls for them to carry more than one load, they have the ability to juggle with ease handling everything all on their own. Given the opportunity when juggling, they are very able and willing to help and see others achieve their goals, which in turn makes them feel good.

When working on their own, it is somewhat easy for them to focus on what they are doing because they have a great sense of vision.

They tend to be quite organized, methodical, systematic and well attuned to details. They do not need to be told how to start a project. They can begin any project themselves with no problem. Expect long hours put in to the task in order to complete the undertaken project. They will complete the job in a thorough and efficient manner because they are very rational, practical and reasonable people. 46/10/1 individuals can take any situation and work with it on their own, which helps them create their own stability.

46/10/1 individuals are service oriented and would do well in business. They possess discipline and patience. Working hard and using their analytical skills is a tremendous asset for them. Although their energies do not attract money, their willingness to work hard helps them achieve their goals, allowing them to hold and organize their finances in an efficient manner.

However, if they lose sight of their positive energies, they easily become emotional, bitter, angered, frustrated, disorganized, confused and openly rigid. They will give the impression or even express that they feel alone or need to be alone. They will be reluctant to help others in achieving their goals and more likely become dependent upon another instead of dependent upon themselves.

Filled with love and appreciation, when it comes to home and family issues, they tend to fit in well since they usually love children and work very well with them. Rarely concerned with material possessions, they thrive on helping others in their own way, thinking on their own, not so much with the opinions of others. They would definitely create a comfortable and stable home life whereby they could build a strong family home. They possess the nurturing qualities to deal with issues in the home and the patience of raising children.

If negative influences happen to impede progress in a relationship, the relationship will suffer because of their instability, lack of discipline, confusion and extreme emotional feelings. Their rigid and stubborn views will in fact make it hard for them to see the whole picture in a relationship, and then make it even harder for commitment to play a stable role in the relationship. As long as they feel that they can control what ever task comes about in their relationship, and that they can make practical advancements, then they will do well.

Notes & Calculations

_____

_____

_____

_____

_____

_____

_____

_____

_____

_____

_____

_____

_____

_____

_____

Notes & Experiences

2

The
Cooperative
Group

Compatible Soulmate, Business Partner, Spouse and Lover

Persons born on the 2nd, 11th, 20th or 29th of an given month, or with a destiny number that adds up to the number 2, is a two person, (For example, someone born on October 20th: 2 + 0 = 2). A number two person communicates devotion best when working in a group.

Color: Orange

Gem: Moonstone

Crystal: Rutile

Planet: Moon

Day of the Week: Monday

Traits

The two person is considerate, cooperative, kind, innovative, creative and loving. These people are highly attuned to the feelings of others; to their predicaments and environment. Therefore, they need choose carefully those they would call a "friend" and that which they would call "home".

The number two is the original "diplo-mat", having an ability to perceive both sides of a circumstance impartially. They are a natural judge since they can listen to opposing arguments neutrally and then make a clear and impartial decision. They listen with equal attention to both the defendant and accuser. Even if they have been in the exact same situation which is before them, they can still remain unbiased.

Not always high in self-esteem and feelings of self-worth, over sensitivity to personal criticism and shyness play a major role in their lives. It is for this reason that they are happier when part of a team, rather than leading a task force, organization or company. They prefer to blend into their surroundings, working quietly to make another person's ideas become a reality. Number two persons have a deep love of song, harmony and all that relates to music and musical instruments. Rhythm is a part of their very soul, and they feel music as well as listen to it.

Career

Interesting areas of employment for the number two person are statesman, ambassador or minister, since diplomacy is an art form. They "make the peace" wherever they go. Often those weary of strife and dissent will go to them for a solution. Their very presence lends a calming effect upon the rough waters of life.

Patience, collaboration and teamwork are practically art forms to them. If they master these arts, they will notice that even at an early age they are eagerly sought out as a valuable member of any committee. Possible career choices for the number two person are as book-keepers, auditors, clerks, instrumentalists, composers, politicians, missionaries, computer experts, pastors or preachers. They are at peace with themselves while they are making peace between others.

Compatibility

Love, companions and alliances are of utmost significance to the number two. Two is an intuitive and willing listener to anyone with problems. They always offer a "shoulder to cry on". The number two must not be alone. It is within their very makeup to be part of a "two-some", otherwise they can become unhappy.

This person seeks association, partnership, craves love and understanding. They are able to follow much better than lead. They like comfort, but are not ambitious. They tend to become a part of a middle class comfort, not an upper class comfort.

They are friendly, but watch it! They tend to be overly sensitive, too emotional, and end up giving love and affection too freely. They seek marriage and companionship to the exclusion of all other life quests, and the desire to be a "duo" is very strong. Divorce often plagues this number as their spouse may feel he/she is shouldering all of the responsibilities without support and input from them. They must work positively to maintain a good relationship especially in marriage. The number two person is not great at expressing themselves, and this is a major cause of divorce for the number 2. Therefore, the number two should refrain from marrying young. This is primarily proven for those born on the 29th of the month.

Therefore, the two person must select their spouses, lovers and companions with exceptional prudence. Their tendency is to be less boastful, conceited or pushy than a number one person. Their credo is tranquillity, devotion and unanimity, and they live up to these ideals throughout life.

They will best agree with those born in the months of May, July, August and October, and with those born on dates adding up to the numbers 1, 4, 6 or 7. Those born in the months of January, April and November will clash with the number two and cause them antagonism. This is also the case with those born on dates adding up to the numbers 8 and 9.

20/2

2: Cooperation and Balance
0: Amplified Gifts and Resources

Color: *Orange*
Gem: *Moonstone*
Crystal: *Rutile*
Planet: *Moon*
Day of the Week: *Monday*

Introducing individuals who may have coined the term the "dynamic duo". For they are very sociable and work exceptionally well with others. Whether working in a team oriented environment or being a part of a social group, they tend to shine and be noticed by those surrounding them. Cooperation is a key to their success, and when their energy is harnessed positively, not many type of people can work in a cooperative manner as well as they can. That is why when they recognize their talents, they will more and more prefer working as a team player instead of being a sole proprietor in any venture they become involved in.

Whenever a situation arises between two opposing parties, expect this person to appear with possible solutions. When they detect discord between two people, bet that the best person to mediate the situation will be the 20/2 person. This is why many of them can be considered and play the role of a diplomat. Remember, these individuals are the team players who work well with others, and are very attentive and sensitive to the feelings of others. Helping others reach their goals is one of their best attributes.

If you find yourself in a relationship with this person, they will give their all to you in the beginning; making the partner feel pleasant, and wanting to be in their company often. No need to worry if these individuals have a heart. They are very sensitive to the feelings of others and tend to show their affection when called for in their relationships.

When given an assignment or starting a relationship, they can be considered good with details. They work as well when continuing a project as they did at the beginning. They will even give you their ear and concentrate on helping you instead of helping themselves. Doors will open with a red carpet, as they give you help. However, when things become too emotionally stressful they will turn away from the entire situation without warning.

Classic co-dependents, their nerves become a factor in any situation once they begin to feel lonely. Oversensitive to personal criticism, these individuals are famous for taking words from others to heart. They experience rapid and deep moods of depression, usually from feelings of loneliness. Also, they tend to do their best to hold in such feelings. Remember, they are not the greatest at expressing themselves.

Once they become tired, bored or unfocused with something or someone, they will begin to become uncooperative or even withdraw from the entire relationship. It could be considered a shield, for after a period of time of giving their all, they become alert to the fact that they may become hurt if a breakup is near. However, don't expect for them to express their feelings to you early in the relationship. The focus of their attention will be on you, the partner. They will give and give, but if they begin to ever feel that they are giving too much or not receiving enough in return, they may become cold, intolerant, resentful, or angry and unaffectionate.

Notes & Calculations

Notes & Experiences

2

3

The
Communication
Group

Compatible Soulmate, Business Partner, Spouse and Lover

Persons born on the 3rd, 12th, 21st or 30th of any given month, or a destiny number that adds up to a number 3, is a number three person. (For example, someone born on May 12th: 1 + 2 = 3). The number three communicates their love from the emotional and passionate side of their personality.

Color: Yellow

Gem: Topaz

Crystal: Galena

Planet: Venus

Day of the Week: Wednesday

Traits

The three personality is ruled by one of three states of mind: the intellectual state, the passionate state or the social state. They usually learn early in life which of these three is dominant in their character. They are friendly, outgoing, warm and have a very social type of personality. They need to and should express themselves at all costs. The three person seeks happiness, beauty in people, and all of their surroundings.

They can demonstrate outstanding creativity in all situations, whether they are at work or at leisure. Satisfaction, beauty and love will surround them always, provided they do not let the negative aspects of their number dominate them. A small bit of childhood demeanor always remains within the number three personality. This is not to say that they are immature, but rather that they have the zest for living and loving that only a pure, unspoiled youth has.

Creativity is basic to their nature in all forms: verse, speech making and even theater work. Never at a loss for words, either spoken or written, their mind has a razor's edge to it. Rarely does anyone "pull the wool" over their eyes. Their quickness of intellect, many perceptiveness and points of view make the three person an accomplished learner.

Since they can be considered to have the traits of visionaries, they have the talent to see the potential in all ideas. In fact, many ideas originate with them. Their vivid imagination lends itself well to many fields, not the least of which is the entertainment field. Monetary rewards can be plentiful if that is their chosen path.

In the negative: they need to try to guard against being too redundant and talkative in their speaking manner. They may divulge more information than they want or need to. This can lead to loss of friendships, as some around them may feel they cannot keep a secret or be trusted with important news.

Some may think of them as sarcastic and nonchalant about serious situations. This is because they are not a worrier and do not worry over minor details. They save their uneasiness for when it is really needed. Loneliness and strife tend to surround them if they do not keep them at bay. Since this is the number of communication and most three's can talk their way out of a bag, they must learn to use this to offset loneliness and potential strife. They are masters of the fast life and can be superficially clever. Three individuals instinctively seek out who and what is most useful to their scheme of the moment, and are sure to make use of what is sought.

Quite often the three may lose their sense of self and this can become a source of misery. They tend to be nervous, restless, capricious and comprised by desires going in several different directions at the same time. The three thinking process sometimes overrides their ability to feel what is right or good, and therefore they must train their mind to work for them rather than against them.

Still, they are ruled by Jupiter's influence and will always be blessed with a fun loving personality, excellent perceptivity of all situations and a superior mind with which to make their fortune. The three personality is strong, determined, resilient, and does not like the feeling of being tied down. In this, they are very similar to the one person.

Positions in life where the three will be a junior assistant or underling will not sit well with them. Taking orders and all the friction that accompanies it will soon have them walking out the door. They are model workers, and perform their tasks in an exemplary fashion. They seek to outdo all those around them and for this very reason, they are set apart from the average worker.

Career

The three should, ideally seek employment in the areas of government, theology or the humanities field. Community standing and reputation are of utmost importance needs to them, and they will never compromise these principles. Possible career choices for the three are writers, public speakers, mimes, performers, comics, cosmeticians or even as salesmen; because with their gift of "gab", selling comes naturally to them.

Relationship

Occasionally, love can be evasive for the number three. Similar to the number one, the three person desires to "climb the corporate ladder of success" with determination and perseverance; sometimes to the detriment of their relationship with their partner. The number three can be dictatorial with those they care for, and ultimately turn their loved ones away from them. The number three is a "name dropper" and will naturally gravitate towards someone of position and power who has made a name for themselves.

They are assigned to the planet Jupiter, and ruled by the planet Venus. They will be most compatible with those born in March, April, May, November or December and with those born on dates adding up to the numbers 3, 6 and 9. Those born in the months of February, June, August and September may cause the number three problems. This also applies to those born on dates adding up to the numbers 4 and 5. The third day of the week, Tuesday, is their best day.

39/12/ 3

3: Expression and Sensitivity

9: Integrity and Wisdom

1: Independence and Confidence

2: Cooperation and Relation

Color: *Yellow*

Gem: *Topaz*

Crystal: *Galena*

Planet: *Venus*

Day of the Week: *Wednesday*

Born to inspire and teach by example, these are individuals who bring out their best when expressing themselves and their sensitivities through their heart. Once they believe in their heart that what they are doing is good and righteous, then their wisdom will take over. Whether they are working independently or in a group, their decisions will most likely be of those acknowledged for its soundness and uniqueness. Spiritual in nature, these individuals have a great aura about themselves when it comes to helping other people. Their expression of feelings, intensifies their relationships socially as well as in business.

Generous, idealistic and compassionate, they set positive examples when in front of others. Occasionally, they experience situations with trivial or superficial matters that tend to impede their progress. Their unique combination of energies may have them become involved in many dramatic situations that may cause their over sensitivity to take control of them. Rarely do they ask for much, therefore they can be content with minimal return for themselves. They are better at working to be humanistic, which is the helping of others.

When they are reluctant to work with other people, their relationships tend to suffer. They spend too much time trying to analyze for themselves instead of concentrating on what is at hand. If their energy is blocked, they can begin to feel overwhelmed and ready to withdraw from a situation; although not without expressing way they feel. This in part because, they lost sight of being in touch with themselves. Since these individuals have an intense independent creativity about themselves, many of their negative experiences are mentally created when they really should have never came about in the first place. Usually many times after they have found that they have given too much of themselves.

30/3

3: Expression and Sensitivity

0: Amplified Gifts and Resources

Color: *Yellow*

Gem: *Topaz*

Crystal: *Galena*

Planet: *Venus*

Day of the Week: *Tuesday*

In many ways, these individuals bring joy, understanding, compassion and service into the world all through their special talents. Very in touch with their own emotions, they are very aware and in tune with whatever venture they choose to take on. Such emotions help others feel a sense of sensitivity from these individuals to the point that many people are inspired by their actions. Not to worry, for their emotions do not control them. However, they just honestly display their feelings and needs when necessary, and unique ways of getting their point across.

If not careful, the 30/3 they can become overly sensitive and have their emotions control them. Due to insecurities, they hide themselves behind by controlling others as if they were puppets. If they have a tendency to complain about the ills that surround them and those in society, it is because they are not sure of themselves. When their energies are tied up in emotional turmoil, they can even expect promiscuous activity that can lead into even deeper emotional turmoil; eventually afflicting their health.

These individuals will give you the shirt off their back if they get to know your needs, and will not expect much in return. Their greatest gift in giving is their emotional support. Of course not everyone wishes to give their true nature away, however, behind that disguise are sharing individuals. Appearing opposite of what they normally are, these individuals can appear fulfilled instead of needy, uncaring, insensitive and unemotional. Spend same time with them, and you will be able to see that they are full of sensitivity and in many cases, giving.

Positively, they can enhance any relationship because they can make their partner feel really loved, all through their emotional, caring and sensitive ways. They are capable of making romance in any relationship. Falling in love is quite easy, and because of this, they become hurt just as easily. Problems arise when determining if they really feel in love with the person or if it is just lust or infatuation. It usually leads to personal mental conflicts.

Attention is very important to this type of person. Many of them are hypersensitive to criticism and need to be handled gently. Self doubt is a big issue and giving them a feeling of security in love matters, makes them come out their shell and express themselves well. They can otherwise become whiners, complainers, and often criticize their mate or partner when working in the negative.

They are great with the written and verbal language, and can express their talents very well. Proper communication to others will always bring strong ties or social connections to these individuals. The only thing that may stop that from happening is when they block their self expression, sensitivity and self doubt.

21/3 & 12/3

2: Cooperation and Balance

1: Independence and Confidence

3: Expression and Sensitivity

Color: *Yellow*

Gem: *Topaz*

Crystal: *Galena*

Planet: *Venus*

Day of the Week: *Wednesday*

Consider the 21/3 creative team players, confident and extremely sensitive. What a combination? These individuals work well with other people. No, they are not necessarily pioneers, but if it is a team project or a relationship that truly requires equal work on all ends, they will definitely be able to handle their end. So sensitive, that they are not great with criticism, but are creative when expressing their emotions and feelings directly to another.

These individuals, like all people, need to work in the positive. For if they do not, they find themselves uncooperative, oversensitive, doubtful and lacking in creativity. Great at giving their all, but if something turns them off or hurts them, they are quick to withdraw. In many cases, they withdraw completely without a partner ever knowing the reason why. Emotions run high and are suppressed within them. Only time and analysis of them may give their partner a better understanding of them, and why they think the way they do. Most of the time, they fluctuate by thinking with their mind one day, and their heart the next.

In a relationship, things are at best when you find them expressing themselves and bringing out their emotions. Controlling their expressions and sensitivity is not one of their greatest attributes. This all comes from an insecurity feeling that they wish to hide from their partner. Concern of expression tends to be more important to them than for their partner. They will without hesitation, test their partner just to see if they should express their feelings regarding emotions of happiness, anger, or pain. They want to know if they are really recognized by their significant other.

If their partner recognizes such, then the 21/3 will become at ease, and give their all in the relationship. However, careful what is said or done to these individuals, for their tendency to be oversensitive can help them withdraw completely without remorse or explanation.

48/12/ 3

4: Practicality and Stability

8: Abundance and Power

1: Independence and Confidence

2: Cooperation

3: Expression and Sensitivity

Color: *Yellow*

Gem: *Topaz*

Crystal: *Galena*

Planet: *Venus*

Day of the Week: *Wednesday*

Ambitious and self confident, they possess good business skill qualities, which are inherent in these individuals. They are very service oriented and would do well in a business of their own. If in charge of an organization or company, manager or leader of a project, they are very practical in their approach to a task. Working long and hard hours while using their analytical skills is a tremendous asset for them. They stand out as being well rounded, thorough and efficient; and if given the option, they work well whether they are alone or in a group.

In facing many rocky roads in their endeavors, they always find a way to create stability. Money is not the most important thing in their lives, and this is not to omit that it helps them, but they do not have a problem attracting money. They may not even be rich, but resources usually will be plentiful for them.

If however, their energies are not in sync in a positive manner, then expect that they will feel very insecure to authority giving them direction, as well as a feeling of being disorganized and confused. Work product usually becomes lacking and inefficient, without any systematic approach for which they are great at.

Relationships will suffer because of their instability and tendency to feel as though they wish to stray from a commitment; both of which can lead to total chaos. Their rigid and stubborn views will in fact make it hard for them to see the whole picture in a relationship, and become oversensitive to personal criticism.

As long as they feel that they can control whatever task comes about in their work or relationship, and that they can make practical advancements, they will of course do well. They are great family makers and are very capable of building a strong home. Usually, they tend to want to lead the relationship and direct how things should be. Call it controlling, if you wish. They could be very loving and affectionate, paying close attention to details of the relationship and lend a shoulder to cry on. This is so, because they have a very sensitive side about themselves.

Notes & Calculations

_____

_____

_____

_____

_____

_____

_____

_____

_____

_____

_____

_____

_____

_____

_____

_____

_____

_____

_____

_____

_____

_____

_____

Notes & Experiences

4

The Group
of Stability
and Order

Compatible Soulmate, Business Partner, Spouse and Lover

Persons born on the 4th, 13th, 22nd or 31st of any given the month, or with a destiny number that adds up to a number 4, is a number four person. (For example, someone born on February 13th: 1 + 3 = 4). They display their love sensually and mentally.

Color: Green

Gem: Emerald, Green Jade

Crystal: Tinstone

Planet: Saturn

Day of the Week: Thursday

Traits

There will never be anyone they meet who will not have the highest compliments to pay them for their dependability, resourcefulness and hard working personality. Others may be unreliable and inconsistent, but not the number four. Number four persons are rooted on solid ground and although they may never invent anything to rival Einstein, they can be a

4

credit to whatever work force they are a part of. Number four persons will win points for sheer stability and endurance. By the same token, their endurance can translate easily into obstinacy and inflexibility, never yielding to another's opinion or point of view. They should not allow this to happen, for they will forfeit many friendships this way.

They tend to be self centered at times, and less than trusting of their fellow man. They must try to avoid this temptation, for basically others are good, not evil. They should avoid getting caught under this wet blanket of negative emotional attitudes which won't allow them to expand.

Since they are ruled by the planet Saturn they have depth and emotional power. It is just a matter of quieting their negative side to allow this positive force to overflow and win at anything! Classic traits of this number are deeds fulfilled through sheer will power, outstanding performance and tenacity. The character of the four person is to be vigilant and contemplative. They don't make a move until all their choices have been considered.

When in the middle of an intense debate, their opinion will usually be the opposite of the popular opinion and, that may cause others to become alienated from them. Deep depressions can be frequent for the person born under the four, since their self-esteem is easily torn down. They tend to be high strung and often will end up with hurt feelings because of this characteristic.

The four enjoys an analytical, mechanical and ingenious mind, as well as boundless optimism. They have a affinity for people who are considered to be idiosyncratic and unique, for they themselves like to be considered different. Society's rules and restrictions hold no allure for the four person and they try to defy them every chance they get.

Career

The armed forces would greatly appreciate having them among their ranks. Fours are highly regimented, disciplined and public spirited, and these are all traits valued by people in uniform. Even if they don't choose to enlist, there are several other fields where their talents

4

of organization, regimentation and concentration would be prized. Number four persons should consider seeking employment in construction, agriculture, politics, machine repair, architecture, secretary, bank clerk, superintendent, law enforcement or manager. Generally, any field where they can use their talent for being systematic is where their real strength lies.

They are methodical in their thoughts; planned and precise in their actions. Some would call them calculating, but this not true. They are just living up to their nature. The only things they "calculate", are how to get the job done in the most efficient manner. Hard work, manual or mental, does not frighten them off. In fact, they relish a day doing a job they can "sink their teeth into" by being busy from start to finish. The day moves quickly for them when they are occupied. They cannot tolerate inactivity; especially their own!

This number craves order and therefore loves tradition. Four persons are steady, almost compulsive about being punctual in all situations, whether they are at home or at work. Four persons both give and demand depend-

95

ability. They apply themselves to work with a fervor, and therefore their security, comfort, stability and steady gains are almost assured.

There is a subtle, inspirational and sometimes quiet mystique about them. The four person's sensitivity is a most powerful gift, but one which they must learn how to use. Often they want to run from their awareness of situations because it may be too painful for them to bear, but it is in understanding that this pain and fear will leave, bring about positive light. The number four person is extremely intuitive, intelligent and aware of people. Due to these gifts, fours often get depressed. When anyone obtains a little bit of knowledge, it can be a powerful thing, but in their case, having such intelligence can be downright oppressive at times; since they tend to struggle on how to approach handling such knowledge.

Compatibility

The love life and courtships of the number four are usually curious and unique affairs. Those they depend upon the most may disappoint them, and the four may in turn

4

disappoint those closest to them as well. In other words, many of their affairs can be cut and dry. Unconventional, best describes the way in which the number four finds love. It may come out of "left field" or from some other equally unusual place. Still, their feelings can be readily offended and their affections easily hurt.

The number four person is assigned to the planet Uranus and their choice companions are those individuals who are most compatible with those born in the months of February, August and June; as well as with those individuals whose birth dates add up to the numbers 1, 2, 5 and 7. Those born in the months of January, May and October may cause hardships for the number four. Individuals born on dates adding up to the numbers 6 and 8 are also in direct conflict with the four person. The fourth day of the week, Thursday, is their best day.

40 / 4

4: Stability and Practicality

0: Amplified Gifts and Resources

Color: *Green*

Gem: *Emerald, Green Jade*

Crystal: *Tinstone*

Planet: *Saturn*

Day of the Week: *Thursday*

This particular 40/4 energy, has all of the same attributes described above in the basic characteristics. However, a very strong emphasis should be placed on their attributes. In other words, here they are not general, but more specifically emphasized. Give them a task and expect commitment and a methodical approach.

These are individuals that take time and patience, focus on details and follow through in carrying out the task. Very practical is the basic description of their nature. The 40/4 persons are rational people, and tend to take any situation and analyze it thoroughly. Whether in front of you or in private, overall they are able to take on the situation and create stability. Any situation that arises, no need to worry, they usually travel with the motto "No condition is permanent. Things could be worse, but with hard work and patience, this too shall pass."

They are methodical in their thoughts; planned and precise in their actions. The only things they consider when working on a project is how to get the job done in the most efficient manner. Hard work, manual or mental, does not frighten them off. The day moves quickly for them when they are occupied. They cannot tolerate inactivity; and will be quick to move on if they feel stagnant in any way.

This number craves order. They love routine and tradition with such energies, they are more intensive than any other person whose numbers happen to add up to a four. They are steady, almost compulsive about being punctual and regular in all situations, be they at home or at work—so much so that it can be overwhelming and demanding upon others who are not as rigid about order and punctuality. They both give and demand dependability with a style that can almost be considered uniformed or regimented. They apply themselves to work with a fervor and therefore their security, comfort, stability and steady gains are all a part of their make up.

There is a highly spiritual energy within them, which surfaces in many ways for all to see. Their organization skills and disciplined focus are powerful gifts, and they must learn how to use them effectively. Often they want to run from their awareness of situations because it may be too painful for them to bear. The key for them is to face that reality with a strong conviction that they have a choice that will help them alleviate such anxiety.

With these gifts, if not careful, they often get depressed. When such depression sets in, it can potentially be on a very deep level, and their mood swings can be very pivotal if it involves questioning their work product. One should not be surprised if in such an emotional state they wish to be by themselves for a long time.

However, their energies must be positive in order to make goals and achievements come to fruition. Otherwise, expect their analysis of dilemmas and situations to be irrational, disorganized and confusing. Relationships will suffer because of their instability, leaving their partner with few options. Their rigid and stubborn views will in fact make it hard for them to see the whole picture in a relationship, and then make it even harder for commitment to play a role in their relationship. In other words, they may tend to stray every now and then if you do not keep their mind focused and hands working on something. Not necessarily labor intensive, but anything work or leisure related that keeps them from inactivity.

As long as they feel that they can control whatever situation comes about in their relationship, they can make practical advancements in the relationship. They are great family makers and are very capable of building a monumental home. This is meant both physically and emotionally. Their partner or companion must keep activity flowing in their lives, and the four will in turn express many of their feelings, emotions and talents.

Anyone involved with this person really needs to observe them and take notice of their talents; for when the 40/4 person is working a positive energy, their companion should acknowledge their talents. This keeps the 40/4 building upon themselves a stronger foundation in which to rest upon. If they are not recognized, only time is needed for them to create their own depression and instability. Then what they have worked so hard to build will begin to crumble.

A willingness to work long and hard hours, coupled with their analytical skills, are tremendous assets for them. Although their energies do not attract money, their willingness to work hard helps them advance in life. They can hold and organize their finances in a very efficient manner. Service oriented persons by nature, they would do well in a business setting or factory work. They usually feel the most rewarded when helping others because they can step back and take a look at the end product that they themselves worked long and hard to build. People cannot appreciate enough the work that number fours do. Four persons are tremendous enablers in helping others achieve their goals.

31/4 & 13/4

3: Expression and Sensitivity

1: Independence and Confidence

4: Practicality and Stability

Color: Green

Gem: Green Jade

Crystal: Tinstone

Planet: Saturn

Day of the Week: Thursday

The 13/4 possesses a great deal of inner strength, both mentally and physically. Taking charge of a situation is not much of a problem for them, and when able to lead, they do it with practicality. Their strong managerial and administrative capabilities become quite apparent with this individual's dedication towards working hard. They have great potential for accomplishment. Financial reward often finds its way into their lives; a blessing within their talents. However, they should not always look for instant rewards, for many times they will find that their working capabilities and potentials can end up latent in application.

With strong personal needs and desires, they should work in the positive and refrain from a dependence on others and other's opinions. If they follow their own convictions they will usually be amazed at the results. Doing this leads to many positive outcomes since they have the talents to do many things on their own. 13/4 people are very rational, independent in nature, and they tend to take any situation and analyze it, helping them to keep stability among themselves, work and family.

Since they tend to be self-centered individuals, they find themselves often surprised when others display resistance to carrying out a task or project in the systematic or methodical way to which they are accustomed. Aware of the way they conduct themselves, they need to take heed and concentrate on how they can help others achieve in a practical, but positive manner.

The 31/4 and 41/3 are ambitious people, but when working in the negative, they lack stability, sensitivity, and patience, ultimately becoming confused and lacking in efficient completion of tasks required of them. Caught between mixed emotions and constant thought as to how they should handle situations, it becomes difficult to balance and make rational decisions. Then the self doubt and tremendous frustration settles in, making them feel dependent upon people or possibly ill warranted substances.

This person does prefer to take the lead in a relationship. However, it is not so much a control issue. They are never afraid of trying new and unique things, for they are creative trendsetters. They believe in working long and hard hours and work in the same fashion towards building a strong relationship. As long as they feel that they can control any situation that comes about in their relationship, they can make practical advancements to harness their talents and the talents of others.

There is no problem attracting friends and colleagues since their personality is filled with warmth and sincerity. A word of caution: Often they tend to express themselves to others in negative ways, and this is a how they express their own insecurities. However, deep down inside, they tend to struggle with being more open with others in the best way they know how, and confess their inabilities to search for the positive. Talking things out with others usually helps them cope with things that plague them.

Great family makers, they are very capable of building a strong home. They bring out the joys of living in their relationships. With their type of creative imagination, they are able to start with nothing or very little, and turn the relationship into something that becomes very romantic or prosperous.

Notes & Calculations

Notes & Experiences

5

The
Freedom
Group

Compatible Soulmate, Business Partner, Spouse and Lover

Those born on the 5th, 14th , or 23rd of any given month, or has a destiny number that adds up to the number 5, is a number five person. (For example, someone born on May 14th: 1 + 4 = 5). They convey love both in a tangible and sensual manner.

Color: *Turquoise*

Gem: *Turquoise, Aquamarine*

Crystal: *Muscovite, Hornblende*

Planet: *Mars*

Day of the Week: *Tuesday*

Traits

This person is usually jovial, fun to be with, and will always be surrounded by comrades. This is because they have a winning way with people and find it easy to acquaint themselves with others. They love travel and freedom, and "variety is the spice of life" is their motto. The five person cannot get enough of voyages to far off places if they get the chance, as well as frequent changes in their own environment.

Independence is their prime concern and they seek it out relentlessly, often at the expense of those around them. Their mental capacities are vast, and they should seek lifetime work using such capacities as opposed to manual labor; where such a gift of intelligence would be diminished. Their choice of friends and associates should be done with extreme prudence; because even though they are versatile in all situations, they may tend to be impulsive and choose wrongly. Their words and deeds must be carefully thought through, so as not to make any capricious decisions in life.

The number five person, unless negative past experiences are involved, strongly feels that sexual expression is a driving force in their life. Their disposition is both powerful and voluptuous. The number five is alluring to the opposite sex for external as well as internal reasons. Physically, they are beautiful, sometimes falling into relationships unknowingly: having people involved with them only because of their looks. Emotionally they are usually good spirited.

The five person needs freedom to express themselves in their love lives, and for this very reason, they may find that life holds more than one marriage for them. Give the number five enough rope to wander and roam where they wish, but rest assure, they will always come back to the person they love. Most of the time, they never really strayed too far in the first place. If they appear to have wandered, they must never know that the rope is there pulling them back to shore. Since they find it difficult to settle down, they must carefully consider the age at which they marry.

Impatience can be their downfall, but they can offset this shortcoming because they possess good discipline. They are able to adapt to any type of situation, and they seek many and varied interests. The five person must learn and accept the laws of change, and not stagnate in personal and/or business relationships.

The five person must not abuse the personal freedom they so urgently seek; especially in matters of sexuality. For once it is attained and then abused, it will lead to unhappiness of the worst sort, misery, suffering and loss. Their magnetism makes them highly memorable persons who possesses a great power and wonderful charm. Personality is the five strong point. They can charm the devil himself. Positive, enthusiastic, spirited, dynamic and larger than life is simply the makeup of their nature.

The number five expects the best from themselves and everyone around them. It is this attitude that helps them to realize their dreams. Should they face disappointment, they are dauntless and have a way of transforming disasters into golden opportunities. Five persons are ruled by the planet Mercury, therefore fond of talking and thinking simultaneously: two priceless qualities with which will help them go far in their endeavors. With independence of the highest order, they have a life most of us can only dream about; filled with travel, romance, love, sex and attainment.

Career

They must try to channel their gifts of successful speculation, athletic prowess and fluent conversation into money making propositions. Possible careers for the five personality would be as a salesperson, psychoanalyst, private eye, government agent or even wall street magnate. They need to harness their energy to try new and exciting things to benefit to their advantage. It is in their nature to explore, scout and inquire into uncharted areas which interest them. Who knows? They might be the one to discover the cure for cancer, or settle the first colony on the moon. Both are within their grasp.

Compatibility

The number five will find harmony with those born in the months of May, June and September, and with those persons whose birth dates add up to 1, 4, 6, 7 and 9. (For example, someone born on September 25: 2+5 = 7). Individuals born in the months of January, March and December may be at the root of number five's problems. The same holds true for those born on dates adding up to 3 and 8. Tuesday is their best day.

32/5

3: Expression and Sensitivity

2: Cooperation

5: Freedom and Discipline

Color: *Turquoise*

Gem: *Turquoise, Aquamarine*

Crystal: *Muscovite, Hornblende*

Planet: *Mars*

Day of the Week: *Tuesday*

Very charming, warm and social is the nature of the 32/5 person. These creative individuals are clever and quick thinking on their feet. Whenever in a work situation they work well in teams; for their cooperation makes them shine all the time. Liberty and no restraints are most important to the 32/5. They are multifaceted, with limitless ideas.

Faced with many internal conflicts, they need to remain free; for they have an exaggerated sense of responsibility and tend to worry more often than necessary. So quick thinking are they, that they tend to react from an emotional level. This creates mood swings in the sense that when something is on their mind, it is difficult for them to express what they feel.

Taking responsibilities for themselves and not so much for others will make them much happier in their every day life. Their interactions with other people bring this about. Now, the 32/5 can be shy in the initial stages of a conversation when at a gathering, but once they have found an audience willing to listen to them, they come around. Actually, they come out shining.

If working with a negative energy, they may feel lacking in creative ideas. Basically, they usually find things get better when they seek new adventures in order to replenish their stock of creative thoughts and ideas. Impatience with others tends to interfere in their thoughts, especially when things are not going as smoothly or the way they anticipated. Lack of planning may become their style, and many times will inhibit their creative flow; leading them to make spontaneous decisions. The 32/5 may prove an unwarranted expense from their pocket and those they choose to travel with if, such spontaneous decisions are made. In other words, their rash and impetuous actions can sometimes backfire, making their road in life very difficult to travel. These are traits they should keep in check.

In relationships, they do well when with someone who gives them freedom, shows love, appreciation and sensitivity for them. Sure, all people probably note that they can use all of the above, however, this person is more sensitive to these needs than most. They are sensitive to feelings of others, especially when it comes to criticism of themselves from another. They take things to heart quickly, which coupled with emotional energies, makes them feel very vulnerable and easily hurt. Usually faster than the next person, they feel this way. This is because their quick energy makes them think about things on a faster level.

These individuals will give you the shirt off their back if they get to know your needs, and will not expect much in return. Just make sure they are not restrained in any manner, and that they are free to go about helping you in the way they feel is best. Their greatest gift in giving is their emotional support.

Of course not everyone wishes to give their true nature away; for they are human too.

Behind that facial disguise are sensitive emotional characteristics. Appearing opposite of what they normally are, these individuals can appear fulfilled instead of needy, uncaring, insensitive and unemotional.

Positively, they can enhance any relationship and make their partner feel really loved, all through their emotional and sensitive ways. They are indeed loving individuals. Whatever the circumstances, these individuals should not be smothered. Remember however, space is needed to keep them happy; otherwise they will end up divorced in record time.

Creating romance in any relationship is easily done. Falling in love is quite easy for them, and because of this, they tend become hurt just as easily. Basically, problems arise in determining if they really feel in love with the person or if it is just lust or infatuation.

41/5 & 14/5

4: Practicality and Stability

1: Independence and Confidence

5: Freedom and Discipline

Color: *Turquoise*

Gem: *Turquoise, Aquamarine*

Crystal: *Muscovite, Hornblende*

Planet: *Mars*

Day of the Week: *Tuesday*

Here are individuals who do not waste time mourning away over the past. These individuals possess much inner strength and take leadership seriously in making plans for the future; making them forever one step ahead of their peers and themselves! No moss gathers on a rolling stone, and these are rolling stones. With these type of individuals, expect that they are rational, independent and practical thinkers.

Even though they tend to move too quickly and are on to new ventures before the ink is dry on their present ones, they are practical and rational enough to justify their actions. They do not pack, plan or make reservations before a vacation; and when they go, they are very organized and efficient with their money. Expect them to be the type to just pick up and leave without notice. To them, that's no problem.

If however, their energies are not in sync in a positive manner, then expect that their analysis of situations to be irrational, disorganized and confusing. Relationships will suffer because of their instability, and it will make the relationship unstable; causing their partner significant grief and stress. Their rigid and stubborn views will in fact make it hard for them to see the whole picture in a relationship, and then make it even harder for commitment to play a role in the relationship.

As long as they feel that they can control what ever task or project that comes about in their relationship, they can move on in a practical manner. They are great family makers and are very capable of building a strong home.

They are at their best when they work as service oriented persons. They would do well in the area of business, because they have great executive and administrative qualities about themselves. Independent and hard working, their sharp and clever minds enable them to use their talents of analytical skills. Although their energies do not attract money, their willingness to work hard helps them. With the money they do make, they can hold and organize their finances in a very efficient manner. They really don't need any help from others.

In a relationship, once they have learned to have more patience with their companion, they need to pay particular attention to details involved in their relationship; otherwise they can become quite erratic. The 14/5 person has the energy and quality of harnessing positive characteristics. This will help build a strong foundation in settling down and possibly starting a family. They are very conscientious in all that they do, however not as emotional as many other numbers. They tend to think and feel from the mind instead of using their heart in matters of love.

Responsible and dependable is their style, and when they attain self discipline, they give all their attention to the relationship with a commitment. Remember, they do need their space to be free. Change and freedom to experience change is what actually exhilarates them. They make a delightful companion, because they are fun to be with. If you plan to go out with one, you definitely better be ready to become involved in many different events or activities when dating or working to grow a business.

Notes & Calculations

_____

_____

_____

_____

_____

_____

_____

_____

_____

_____

_____

_____

_____

_____

_____

_____

_____

_____

_____

_____

_____

Notes & Experiences

_____

_____

_____

_____

_____

_____

_____

_____

_____

_____

_____

_____

_____

_____

_____

_____

_____

_____

_____

_____

_____

_____

_____

_____

_____

124

The Group
of Balance,
Responsibility,
Vision,
and Love

Compatible Soulmate, Business Partner, Suitable Spouse and Lover

Individuals born on the 6th, 15th and 24th of any given month, or with a destiny number that adds up to a number 6, is a number six person. (For example, someone born on May 24th: 2+4 =6). They exhibit deep emotional feelings, that come directly from the heart.

Color: Blue

Gem: Blue Sapphire, Blue White Pearl, Diamond

Crystal: Indicolite

Planet: Jupiter

Day of the Week: Sunday, Monday, Friday

Traits

Showing love, companionship, and association with others earns high marks with the number six person. Expressing parental love comes more naturally than sensual love. Appreciation and affection is of prime importance because of their high emotional order. This individual is usually handsome and captivating, and attracts the opposite sex fairly easily.

This is the number which loves family and home. They seek to be a peacemaker and are usually found to be very understanding. They are compassionate listeners, with a ready ear for the problems of others. Number six born individuals do not shy away from responsibility and seek to take charge of that which is entrusted to them.

They adjust well to all situations and the warning is strong against divorce, as this opposes their very nature. Strife, failure and unwanted obligations can result from not paying strict attention their inner yearnings. Family and harmony must come first.

Authority, a happy home, an outstanding marriage, security and material wealth can be theirs for the taking. This is largely due to their being conscientious and responsible nature. Usually, their competence is never questioned. Instead, it is assumed. Therefore, they are often the most valued employee in the workplace.

The single most important challenge to the six is to avoid being a nit-picking perfectionist.

They often see flaws where none exist. They tend to underestimate themselves as well as those around them. This can be infuriating to their acquaintances. They must try to put this fault to rest.

Highly intelligent, the number six individual possess a clever and sarcastic sense of humor and can have fun simply for fun sake. They are kind and caring, and can be a substantial force in the face of sickness, death and severe depression. They are ruled by the planet Venus, and passion is almost a religious experience for them. The pull of the Goddess of Love is very strong.

Career

They will be surrounded by good companions all their lives, as they find it exceptionally easy to make and keep friends. They are Epicureans, fond of all the arts and the finer things in life. The six person will find happy employment in the areas of design and fashion, painting, artistry, medicine, interior design, culinary studies, education, music or investment banking. As long as their life takes on a predictable nature, regardless of their profession, they will be happy. The six person is a natural homemaker and takes delight in making others always feel welcome. Harmony and accord beset them. It is contagious, as those around the six flock to them; knowing they will be warmly received.

They cannot abide by envy or dissension. The six is very perceptive. They have an uncanny ability to understand other people. In dating such a person, it is possible to win the number six over with lavish displays of thankfulness, recognition and rewards. Six personalities follow the "straight and narrow path" since they have a strong perception of what is morally right and wrong. Never cross swords with the six person, as they would rather die than go against what they firmly believe in.

Compatibility

The six person should avoid an early marriage if possible. If love, great comforts and extreme appreciation are dangled in front of the six, an alliance is almost assured. The number six person will be most suitably matched with those born in the months of May and October; followed in turn by March, April and July. Those born on dates adding up to the numbers 2, 3, 6 and 9 will be compatible with the six person. (For example, someone born on April 20th: 2 + 0 = 2). The number six is assigned to the planet Venus. The sixth day of the week, Friday, is their best day.

However, those born in the months of January, February and August will bring a host of problems with them for the number six. The same can be said of those whose birth dates add up to the numbers 4 and 8.

15/6

1: Independence and Confidence

5: Freedom and Discipline

6: Balance, Responsibility, Vision and Love

Color: *Blue*

Gem: *Blue Sapphire, Blue White Pearl, and Diamond*

Crystal: *Indicolite*

Planet: *Jupiter*

Day of the Week: *Sunday, Monday, Friday*

The 15/6 person focuses on the family and home, but with a twist of independence in their style. Unlike other six individuals, they are not routine in their family functions. They command change and do not allow themselves or family members (if they can help it) to perform monotonous activities.

Clever thinkers and quick on their feet, they express a high level of intelligence in all that they do. They don't need anyone else to help them with a task they choose, whether it be for themselves or for their family. Even being a single parent comes easier for them, if they are forced to be in such a situation. Their confidence tells them that no task is too great pertaining to the home and family.

Making friends is not hard for them, for they are good at expressing themselves. They are independent thinkers and venture out on their own to obtain what they wish; not depending on others or their opinions. When those they love are threatened, they may become defensive or fight for what they believe. When threatened, they can be quick to pick up those they love, without hesitation, and travel to a distant land to be safe.

The 15/6 person in the negative realm, can become quite restless and impatient. Never expect them to stay dormant in any aspect of their lives or the lives of their family, otherwise they will become bored, self indulgent, and lack the discipline to keep themselves and their family together. They may even tend to become quite erratic, and have strong feelings of constraint; inhibiting their clever thinking abilities.

In relationships, they are definitely fun to be with. Emotional beings, they tend to think a little more frequently from their mental or intellectual side as opposed to thinking from their heart. They are willing to work alone, but they do like companionship, as long as they are not being smothered. They are great home makers that add the spice of life and life's experiences to the household. Also, the 15/6 is wonderful at maintaining a home where family members are constantly on the go.

Prepare to go on dates that are not the same old run-of-the-mill, but are filled with exhilarating activity each time you go outside. Remember, a lot of hugs and kisses are in order each time you go out with them, for all six individuals need a lot of love and appreciation.

24/6 & 42/6

2: Cooperation

4: Practicality and Stability

6: Balance, Responsibility, Vision and Love

Color: Blue

Gem: Blue Sapphire, Blue White Pearl, Diamond

Crystal: Indicolite

Planet: Jupiter

Day of the Week: Sunday, Monday, Friday

Careful what is said, especially when criticizing these individuals. They are very oversensitive and emotional. Analytical in their makeup, they tend to analyze everything that is said, especially when it is said about them. They then try to be as rational as possible, when coming to a conclusion about what was meant by the person(s) who made the comment.

Practical in approach, they are by no means independent, but work better in groups. Family and home oriented, they are individuals of habit and routine. In keeping with their nature, they take a systematic, methodical and orderly approach to taking care of the family and home. A sense of order must be a part of their household. With the energies they possess, they are very efficient and deep rooted in building a strong family foundation. They are capable of taking charge and giving direction; helping them and others become strong individuals. These individuals are very good at judging character no matter who they tend to work with, and are very protective of those that they hold closest to their heart.

In relationships, once committed, they are truly great companions and work very hard at a relationship. However, just getting them to be committed can be quite a task. A commitment involves becoming routine in a manner that may not be practical for them. Relationships can to start to become routine, and without change or the ability to display perfection in a relationship because of a settled partner, they will be extremely unhappy. The partner must show some creativity as well as spontaneity.

When in a bad relationship, the 24/6 would be so unhappy that they would lose concentration, lack patience, become confused and disorganized. Instead of showing much affection, which they are very good at doing, it would be just the opposite. Difficulty in attracting wonderful companions can become an issue if they do not work with positive energies. Relationships will suffer because of their instability and a tremendous amount of work would be needed to rectify it. Their actions can be quite rigid and stubborn, which will in fact make it hard for them to see the whole picture in a relationship. Further, it will be even harder for commitment to play a role in their relationship.

When in love, or when they take a liking to a person, they work long and hard to keep a relationship. They will work diligently to build a foundation for both their companion and themselves. It would be very helpful for their companion to work with the number six, encouraging them in all they do. Then, the 24/6 or 42/6 individual begins building or displaying the foundation they put together for the relationship.

In working in the positive, they are best at their talents when they become service oriented persons. Working hard and using their analytical skills is a tremendous asset for them. Although their energies do not attract money, their willingness to work hard helps them achieve stability. They do enjoy the finer things in life, and will take any opportunity to have life provide those things they desire. Once they obtain them, they can hold and organize their finances and luxuries in a very efficient manner; as well as enjoy sharing what they have obtained with their loved one.

Always ready to help, whether for service or a loved one in distress, they lend a kind and sympathetic ear, gentle hand and shoulder to cry on. This person is usually a lover of children, and works well with them. They make their companion very happy to be with them.

6

Notes & Calculations

_____

_____

_____

_____

_____

_____

_____

_____

_____

_____

_____

_____

_____

_____

_____

_____

_____

_____

_____

_____

_____

_____

_____

_____

Notes & Experiences

7

The Group
of Trust
and
Openness

Compatible Soulmate, Business Partners, Spouse and Lover

Individuals born on the 7th, 16th or 25th of any given month, or has a destiny number that adds up to a number 7, is a number seven person. (For example, someone born on August 25th: 2+5=7). They are spiritual in expressing their love.

Color: *Violet*

Gem: *Alexandrite*

Crystal: *Amethyst*

Planet: *Mercury*

Day of the Week: *Saturday, Sunday*

The seven person prefers to live within themselves. They are philosophical, intelligent and intellectual. Known for keeping their inner thoughts to themselves, which can tend to drive those around them to madness. They love to be conservative, and this trait will serve them well. Self restraint, usually keeps them from rushing in where fools dare to tread. Their motto is "go for it, and deal with the consequences later!"

7

They live their lives in the in the clouds, not down on earth; whereby they put themselves above menial work. They are reactionaries and not revolutionaries. That is, they dislike change of any kind and prefer to stay with the tried and true methods of the past. They seek solitude, quiet and meditation, often seeking to live alone.

Above all, faith is their strongest desire. Faith in themselves and faith in others is the focal point of life to them. They always seek understanding and knowledge where the laws of the Creator are concerned, and this is a pleasurable task for them. If they deny their call to faith; poverty of soul, loneliness, misery and unhappiness will follow. Wisdom and knowledge are the keys to remaining true to themselves. The voice that always whispers, "who am I?" must be answered.

The seven has an unsurpassed talent for bringing out the beauty in life. They relish and revel in beauty in all forms and find it everywhere they look. With Uranus as their planetary ruler, they can be sure that they will have a highly perceptive and alert personality;

finely attuned to all of life's subtleties. They put knowledge to its best use, creating for themselves a life of enjoyment, laughter and love.

Their remoteness of nature and unobtrusive style tend to make the seven remain basically to themselves. They may seem stand-offish, but this is only because they can be at times, extremely quiet. "Still waters run deep" and the seven is no exception, since their reserved exterior belies an inner furor of individuality, originality and self-sufficiency. Their love of travel to exotic locations in search of inner serenity is all consuming. The seven is a student of the world; devouring all there is to know around them and therefore enjoys the reputation of a scholar. The seven can be flooded with prophetic visions, whether awake or asleep.

As a scholar, very few people surpass the number seven. They are known for their love of the written word and all affairs of the mind. They will tend to dwell on a subject for what appears to be an interminable amount of time. The seven personality is not trying to bore his or her companions, but rather they are just trying to know a subject well. The only way they can accomplish this, is by pondering an issue at great length.

Due to their learned nature, they tend to disagree often with the opinions of others. Since they feel they are an authority on many matters, sevens don't wish to waste time entertaining the solutions those around them might offer. How can they be correct, is their major internal issue in which the grapple with. They are the "genius" of any crowd. They must try not to be too conceited as this can alienate people quickly. Sevens can be wrong also. No one is perfect.

Since their satisfaction comes from within rather than externally, they are often content to be alone. Usually it is because they have reached a higher plane of understanding themselves. This is a level to which few can rise, but to which the seven rises to rather easily. They have a great knack for introspection and reflections. Inner peace is within their grasp because they have a philosophical nature and can readily accept what happens to them in life.

This does not mean they will lay back and passively allow misfortune to occur, it just means that when unfortunate things do happen, they can rationalize them better than those who fight their fates. They are guided almost intuitively and can call upon their "sixth sense". It rarely fails them and they can make decisions based on hunches when others would be afraid to. They loathe pandemonium and commotion, and will often flee from a boister-ous situation; retreating to the quiet of their own mind. Others would just like to know why they conduct such actions, and can misconstrue this trait in the negative. They are not snobbish, just happy within themselves.

Career

They are people of few words, for they garner much of their information through observation only. Scrutiny and investigation are the trademarks of the seven personality, and therefore they enjoy professions in science, medicine, solitary writing and playing instru-ments. It would also be good to consider their lifetime work in the fields of instruction, mys-tic affairs, invention, law or botany. Private research is their ideal career. They can think, be alone and get paid to do it.

The number seven is family oriented. While the seven person expects and loves to receive gratitude, they find it burdensome to return the favor. Since the seven is so spiritual, but somewhat introverted in relationships, they are inclined to hold in their emotions, beliefs and feelings; instead of relying upon their inner soul to see them through trying times. This is why their marriages and relationships tend to suffer. They tend to look within themselves too much for their solace, and not to their mate for such matters of importance.

Compatibility

The seven is a "laid back" pursuer of the opposite sex. They are quiet and patient in their pursuit of love, but once the right partner is found, they fulfill that person's every need. The number seven is assigned to the planet Neptune. The Seventh day of the week, Saturday, is their best day. The number seven person will be in harmony with those born in the months of February, May, July and August, and with those born on dates adding up to the numbers 1, 2, 4, 5 and 7. (For example, someone born on May 13th: 1 + 3 = 4). Those who are born in the months of January, April and October may cause the seven some adversity. Those whose birth dates add up to the numbers 3, 8 and 9 are likewise not compatible with the seven person.

16/7

1: Independence and Confidence

6: Balance, Love, Responsibility and Vision

7: Trust and Openness

Color: *Violet*

Gem: *Alexandrite*

Crystal: *Amethyst*

Planet: *Mercury*

Day of the Week: *Saturday, Sunday*

The 16/7 individuals possess great vision and independence. They can picture things happening in the future, and are good for carrying through what they see with confidence and acceptance by others. They are not always willing to share what they are thinking, for they fear that some one may try to steal their ideas or vision. However, once they begin to confide in you, they will then reveal new possibilities and endeavors as they express their meaning of truth and beauty.

They think for themselves, and by themselves. Once they have found such unconditional, but not naive trust in themselves and others, they see the inherent perfection in all their possible achievements and future goals. Even in the most uncanny and difficult situation, they find the wonderful powers of a higher being looking out for them. It is this spirit, once they have found it within themselves, that brings the most uplifting and deep understanding of themselves and that of others.

If such energies are favoring the negative, these individuals will tend to feel bitter and betrayed by others. Independence seems to go out the window, and feelings of insecurity blankets their inner thoughts, along with possible self destructive behavior. The 16/7 can really struggle while learning their lesson on this planet. Feeling disappointed and/or frustrated in those they feel they vested so much time and thought into, and that no one has lived up to their expectations, makes it difficult for them to swallow and move on. When critical negative influences arise, these individuals should especially be careful of dependencies such as the abuse of alcohol and drugs.

Through sharing their beauty and appreciation of life, a partner or companion can feel their positive energy and feel a part of their expression they release to the world. Smart individuals, they may show off their talents by taking the lead in the relationship. If they feel threatened in any manner, or unable to lead in the relationship, they can become quite emotional and depressed; while concealing any expression of such.

Analytical thinkers, they look deeply into their relationships to understand their partner in all that they do or say. They will then decide after an analytical breakdown, whether or not they should be open and trusting, and moreover, can they trust the person they begin to care about. Very private in nature, it can take a long time to get to know a seven, and may even be quite frustrating.

A person of true intellect, very few people surpass the mental sharpness of the 16/7. If and when they truly feel a spiritual nature within themselves, they become known for their love of the written word and all affairs of the mind. One moment they love and think with their mind and at other times with their heart. Try and tell them something may be of no use, it doesn't matter; for they are not the kind of people to trust the opinion of others. They are independent minded, question oriented individuals. Remember, they tend to dwell on a subject for what appears to be an insurmountable amount of time; hopefully to get answers or a better understanding of what is at issue.

25/7

2: Cooperation and Balance
5: Freedom and Discipline
7: Trust and Openness

Color: *Violet*

Gem: *Alexandrite*

Crystal: *Amethyst*

Planet: *Mercury*

Day of the Week: *Saturday, Sunday*

True seekers of deep understanding, they usually find what they are looking for in life. However, they always face the question of whether or not they can believe in what they found as an answer. They feel and know there is an inner guidance within them, but are reluctant to follow it. When they do, they are disciplined in following the course laid out before them.

Taking the advice of others, but not solely depending on the advice is their nature. This is because they look inside themselves to find whatever they need to know. Working or just being social, they are very good and respected around people. Analytical, quick thinking, clever and disciplined. Traveling is what they love to do if given the opportunity, and enjoy it if doing it with more than one person.

They respect their own internal feelings and messages. They are willing to take adventures while living the liberated life; feeling comfortable and at home almost anywhere. Embracing inner freedom like a treasure, they feel touched by a sense of oneness; along with peace and inner harmony. These individuals leave a spirit behind them, as if it were a shadow to be admired.

If these individuals in any way become or feel restrained in work or play, they tend to mistrust others, and prefer their own solitude instead of sharing with others. Quickly, they become aimless seekers of experience or avid readers of spiritual books for self-understanding. This is their way of trying to understand what they are going through. They can become introverted, undisciplined, stagnant and unwilling to venture out to new and exciting things. All mostly due to negativity within themselves.

Great companions, freedom oriented, fun loving and spiritual. Keeping these individuals going is the key to a successful relationship. An all night candle and a movie channel is not the only thing on their mind. Travel to far away places is what they look for. Different activities and challenging games is their style. Being around groups of people looking to experience the fun also helps them stay clear of the same old routine. Extremely bright people, they can use their incisive mind in service and support of others. Enhanced by clear ability to think and be creative, skillful hands, anyone who is helped by the 25/7 will feel a positive touch of their spirit when working together.

Keep in mind what you say to these individuals, for they are oversensitive to personal criticism. They tend to experience fears and pain of betrayal, real or imagined, and its all kept inside their head. To have a working relationship, they must trust their mind and think their way through emotions. They need to be more expressive as to what they feel instead of keeping to themselves. Whether with their spouse, lover or partner, you will notice that they desire a high degree of privacy and independence. The 25/7 always looks and seeks harmony, balance and completeness through joining with a partner. This is because they don't always feel the harmony and completeness in themselves.

34/7 & 43/7

3: Expression and Sensitivity

4: Stability and Process

7: Trust and Openness

Color: *Violet*

Gem: *Alexandrite*

Crystal: *Amethyst*

Planet: Mercury

Day of the Week: Saturday, Sunday

Organized, systemic, practical thinkers and doers. Open yourselves to them and expect them to create a strong foundation and base in all that they do. Socialites they can be, this is only if they can overcome the actions of being shy around people they don't know. Shyness can be habit among them because expression is something they need to get a hold of. Once they do, then they can be at any function or organization and gather any audience and their utmost attention.

Sensitive is their nature. Practical, physical and spiritual, these individuals have learned to trust the mystery and wisdom of life working through them, and through everyone else they come in contact with. With all of these energies combined, consider them worldly ones, with a commitment toward inner growth. These individuals are dedicated to their work and willing to work long and hard until the job is complete. They believe in sharing their inner spirit, as long as others are open and trusting with them.

Consider them insightful, and individuals who are connected to the Spirit even while pursuing the practical concerns of everyday life.

If they ever lose focus on what they should be accomplishing, then these individuals may have difficulty in coming to grips with conflicting desires for security and drives to go within themselves in order to escape from the material world. Indecisive and confused, the 34/7 and 43/7 feel as though they have problems with people in general at times, because they are sensitive to people's ordinary trusting nature. Bottom line is not to worry about others, but to worry about themselves and to manage their own lives in a more harmonious manner.

In their relationship endeavors, they are very good at creating stability and constancy. Finding it hard to be committed in their relationships, because relationships last a long time and in some cases can become too routine. They are afraid to accept routine, neglecting the fact that what may happen in their relationships in the future, can be rewarding attributes. This is especially the case if they become very sensitive and guess that they understand everything, or enough to make what they believe to be a firm determination about the relationship. Commitment will not be for them. They need some spice added to their routine.

Mental thinkers they are, and if up to them, they usually remain this way throughout life. What is of utmost important to them is open, honest communication and associated trust in their partner; then they will find that any relationship they are involved in, will in fact thrive. Trust issues center on a subtle, underlying sense of feeling uncomfortable. They are not entirely relaxed when they're with others. It's as if they might say the wrong thing which they sometimes set themselves up to do: whereby if they just concentrate on being themselves, they will not have to worry about that.

Notes & Calculations

_____

_____

_____

_____

_____

_____

_____

_____

_____

_____

_____

_____

_____

_____

_____

_____

_____

_____

_____

_____

_____

Notes & Experiences

8

The Material and Power Group

Compatible Soulmates, Business Partners, Spouse and Lover

Those born on the 8th, 17th and 26th day of any given month, or with a destiny number that adds up to the number 8, is a number eight person. (For example, someone born on May 26th: 2+6 =8). Their expressions of love come from the psychological and analytical side of their character.

Color:	*Rose, Red and Pink*
Gem:	*Diamond*
Crystal:	*Pyrite*
Planet:	*The Sun*
Day of the Week:	*Thursday*

Traits

The eight person is the lover of big business, large accumulations of wealth and material possessions. They seek power, money and huge success. Often enough, they achieve it. They have confidence and courage, and often these are the traits with which they can effectively climb to the top of the corporate ladder.

Eight persons must learn the correct use of power and material objects. They must not become overly concerned with material affairs, though it doesn't hurt to pay attention to them either, especially the details that make up material matters. If they allow themselves to go to extremes in the greed department then ruin, destruction, failure and even catastrophe can result. Eight individuals must turn their natural tendencies as a business person into lasting money, power, position and prestige, not covetousness.

No question, they are an intensely private, strongly secretive and rather suspicious oriented persons. Neither do they reveal themselves to anyone, nor do they form close friendships overnight. They are always looking out. This tends to suggest how they seem to find good business opportunities. These individuals prefer a one on one situation as opposed to a large social gathering, unless it is a forum created by them. When focusing their will, they are an invincible force and can rise above and against all odds. Security seekers, they tend to suffer intensely when the rug is pulled out from beneath their feet; making it hard for them to recuperate. However, they do have a richness of character and a compassionate heart to help them go on.

As Mars is their planetary ruler, the ability to extend themselves is far beyond what is expected of their character. Through sheer stamina and force, one can be sure that all they strive for will never be far from their grasp. First, they must recognize that whatever they desire is obtainable, then no more needs to be said.

The eight is very reflective in all they say and do, and is very careful before making a move of any kind. Life and the unexpected events it holds will never shock the eight, because they are philosophical about all that happens to them and those around them. If given the opportunity, they will be happy in service to the public, and do not mind intrusion in their personal life when making a contribution to society. Their ambition is legend, and because of it they will aim for high ideals. The "vibes" they send out are an enigma, and therefore out of all possible numbers, the eight is perhaps the most often misunderstood.

The eight person will always seem to be at odds with themselves. Others may think they are cold, unfeeling or callous, when in fact, this couldn't be further from the truth. The generous, understanding and sympathetic nature of the eight is unmatched anywhere. Their isolation in life is a direct result of so often being "mis-read" by others. Love for them is expressed with Much passion, fervor and emotion.

Career

They could be the manager of a department, but would be better as chairman of the board. To be a vice president is not enough, preferring the presidency instead. At times, their drive may become so strong they can tend to lose sight of their spirituality. Many times they need to be reminded that without great reflection upon their inner self, nothing is possible. It would most likely be helpful if they could stop and "smell the flowers" every now and then, especially during their climb to the top. They must realize that not everything is all cut and dry. Only in time do things come to fruition.

Their make up naturally helps them find happiness in executive areas, such as an efficiency expert, bank president, capitalist, business mogul or tycoon. If they choose the field of acting, they will win the academy award. They will succeed fabulously in any area they set their sights on. Few people can boast such wonderful credentials. The eight is to be envied.

Relationships

Love is a very deep experience for the eight person, and this is often misunderstood by those involved with them. The number eight is a very sensitive, sympathetic, gentle and an unselfish person. This especially holds true for those closest to the number eight person. Wives, lovers, friends and partners of the eight will delight in the warmth of their relationship. Since they are very reflective and thoughtful, the number eight is usually drawn to persons much older than them.

The number eight is assigned to the planet Saturn and their choice companions are those born in the months of January, March, October and December. Those whose birth dates add up to the numbers 3, 6 and 8 are good companion choices. (For example, someone born on December 15th: 1+ 5 =6). However, those born in the months of February, August, June and are not good companion choices, as are those whose birth dates add up to the numbers 1, 4 and 5. The fifth day of the week, Thursday, is their best day.

17/8

1: Independence and Confidence

7: Trust and Openness

8: Abundance and Power

Color: Rose, Red Pink

Gem: Diamond

Crystal: Pyrite

Planet: The Sun

Day of the Week: Thursday

The working energy of the 17/8 is basically that of independent thought analysts. Leaders in their own right, they are among the few that can actually run a business and not experience much trouble with business operations. The fates and fortune telling are not attractive to the number eight, for they are very hard people to convince. Sometimes, it may seem impossible. They do not believe in being in the right place at the right time, for they believe that there is only a right or wrong. The way to get ahead in life is through the gathering of their own honor stripes. That means hard work on their part. Their fortune tends to come with the feeling that it was self made; with hard work and not luck. One could tell them the world, or even express one of the greatest entrepreneurial ideas in the universe, however, they will still remain leery. They will disbelieve those who claim that they can make it, or have made it in life using hunches and "long shots".

If one looks to be a partner with these individuals, caution! They prefer to work alone. If in fact they change their attitude and are willing to work with someone else, they will place that person under a microscope and analyze them for a greater understanding of where they come from. If they appear aloof and distant, is not because they don't get along with people, it is just that they work differently from most other people. They work on a different

8

level and usually take an alternative approach to tasks, unlike other people.

Eight individuals are difficult people to understand, because they continue to search to find out about themselves. They don't portray any easy perceptions. Just the same, they look at people as though they are complex, which makes it hard for them to trust people and be open with them. They keep themselves busy trying to figure out about others, while usually struggling without knowing, to understand themselves.

If a turn for the worst has occurred in their lives, they can find themselves becoming insecure, withdrawn, afraid of confrontation, and baffled by the world. The 17/8 desires recognition. If they continue on with a negative aura, they will fear betrayal and feel that something is missing; namely the spiritual side of their life. The 17/8 can become obsessed with power, over-controlling, and skeptical about trusting in business affairs. They have a great inner strength, but may end up doubting the faith in the powers of themselves or their so called inner Spirit.

In relationships, they are difficult to get to know, but have glorious personalities; especially once they become comfortable in your presence. They often give out little information about themselves, unless other energies and circumstances command otherwise. Most of these individuals require some time to trust a new partner. They will analyze each and every thing in the relationship to make sure it is going right, whatever right is to them. After a decision is made, they look to be in control of the relationship, for they must be independent in all that they do. That includes their thought process or behavior pattern. Then, and only then, do they open up with the prospects of emotional intimacy.

26/8

2: Cooperation

6: Balance, Responsibility, Vision, Love

8: Abundance and Power

Color: *Rose, Red Pink*

Gem: *Diamond*

Crystal: *Pyrite*

Planet: *The Sun*

Day of the Week: *Thursday*

Cautious movement and many confinements often hinder them. This does not have to be, for they can learn to control the manner in which they move through the world and still be careful without stagnating. They are intellectual persons, and most of their decisions are well thought out and balanced. Spontaneous , rash decisions are easily avoided by their precise calculations.

Their vision of making things happen is very acute, and they can balance more than one task quite comfortably. Most of their success usually comes from cooperating with others who help them find their way to success. They are at their best when teamwork is involved. Their abilities become apparent and well recognized as the one who could be the executive leader, diplomat or a negotiator. Without hesitation, they are capable of taking charge and giving direction, even inspiring others. They are good at judging character no matter who they seem to work with.

Service to others is where their abilities bring them most of their success. Responsible in their deeds, they pick up responsibilities where others falter; better at continuing a task as opposed to starting one. Remember, most eights are not of the independent type. Service to others signifies achievement, but they are not satisfied with ordinary achievement; they are only content with the gusto! Their personality drives them, and they must reach the greatest heights possible in both work and relationships.

These 26/8 individuals are not as concerned with material possessions as some of their eight counterparts. They would rather command the feeling of power in the gathering of masses of people, working with them and providing service for them. Material possessions are nice, but they don't actually fully live their lives for them. Great with words in both the verbal and written sense, many people are attracted to them and appreciate their manner of communication.

If in business, they are efficient when working. You can trust that when given an assignment, they will be professional and thorough. They are very capable of organizing and administrating any business or office. When all positive energies come together, expect that they will be offered a high position; or promoted in the one they already possess; or made partner in a business. They can ultimately build a massive empire.

The 26/8 must keep working in the positive for they will otherwise become too rigid, stubborn, timid, and hard to live with. Furthermore, they judge others by their own standards, and can be somewhat bossy and controlling. They wear a mask to hide their true feelings, and prefer not to express them.

Open and honest, they are devoted partners, companions and spouses who feel most comfortable in a home and family setting. They make good parents and work well with children. They can be very sensitive to your needs, never hesitating to lend you an ear or a shoulder to cry on when things are not going right. Don't forget however, these individuals need a lot of love and appreciation, and can be overly sensitive when it comes to criticism of themselves from another. They do take things to heart. The leadership role in their relationships make them feel best, and unless they are in control, they will feel insecure. Remember, they can be over controlling perfectionists, critical of others, and judge themselves as well as others against unrealistically high standards.

They have the potential to give much love and affection. They have a good head on their shoulders and show much emotion whenever involved in a relationship. They may not be the best at expressing emotion, for they usually hold in their feelings due to a fear of being hurt. They can be hurt very easily.

Ambitious and self confident, they will definitely keep their partner from becoming bored. They tend to feel as though they can tackle anything that comes before them, especially that which may hinder the relationship. They make a great effort to concentrate on the perfect relationship, thinking of loved ones as super human; only to be disappointed when they come across people who are only human.

35/8

3: Expression and Sensitivity

5: Freedom and Discipline

Color: Rose, Red Pink

Gem: Diamond

Crystal: Pyrite

Planet: The Sun

Day of the Week: Thursday

Ask something from them, and you shall receive. They are dependable in mostly all that they do. If they happen to need a hand from someone, they are very good at judging character, and quite capable of determining whether or not they wish for a particular person to work with them in any activity. When they start the activity, they are realistic in the possible achievement of the goal, and are creative in their approach.

Seeking a warm personality? Here is one that is social, warm and friendly. If they have learned to express themselves without being shy, they are great conversationalists, whether at a social gathering or business function. Attracting an audience is never really a problem. As a matter of fact, their energies are so strong that they can attract money much easier than many other people. Rarely do they ever find themselves without money to spend. This is not to say that they should be rich, but they have enough money to be comfortable enough until they are ready to make more.

What makes their energy even more powerful and noticeable is the fact that they have a very creative imagination. Whether they have an empty cup or a drop in a cup, they can make it full faster than most people. Clever and quick thinking, they take advantage of opportunities and find a way to benefit themselves. So versatile are they, that they must always be involved with something or someone new or different and are always looking to improve themselves.

Strong-minded, ambitious and self-confident individuals, they are best able to create wealth through service. They are very capable of organizing and administrating any business or office, and when all energies are working in the positive, they can build a massive empire; expressing great leadership and authority.

When working on a project or taking out time for a relationship, their nature is restlessness and impatience. If quick satisfaction is not received, never expect them to be with one project or person too long without becoming bored. They have no problem in saying good bye to the old and saying hello to the new.

Anything can be achieved with them unless their energies become negative. Then a change for the worse could happen. Typically, it could start with a lack of patience, then actions can become erratic, unrealistic, self-doubtful and stagnant. It is change and freedom to experience life and its gifts which actually exhilarates them.

In their relationships, many 35/8 persons usually find it difficult to keep a long term relationship until they are thirty or forty years old. They have a freedom nature about themselves and an urge to experience life. Life moves on with them, through travel or just a reluctance to settle down. Until they get most of that freedom energy out of their system, they tend to fall into power struggles with their partner. Unless their partner is more submissive than them, they will continue (not so much outwardly) to rebel until that power they desire is obtained. These individuals feel more secure when they feel in control. Issues of dependence or independence will come into play if their partner, companion, spouse or lover fails to recognize that the 35/8 wants to be placed in control.

Notes & Calculations

_____

_____

_____

_____

_____

_____

_____

_____

_____

_____

_____

_____

_____

_____

_____

Notes & Experiences

_____

_____

_____

_____

_____

_____

_____

_____

_____

_____

_____

_____

_____

_____

_____

_____

_____

_____

_____

_____

_____

_____

_____

8

The Honesty
and Wisdom
Group
(The Humanitarian)

Compatible Soulmate, Business Partner, Spouse and Lover

Those born on the 9th, 18th and 27th day of any given month, or with a destiny number that adds up to the number 9, is a number nine person. (For example, someone born on December 27th: 2 + 7 =9). They tend to show their love in a impetuous and devout manner.

Color: *Orange Yellow Gold, Saffron*

Gem: *Opal*

Crystal: *Alum*

Planet: *Planet Assigned, Mars*

Day of the Week: *Monday (Alone), Friday (With Companions)*

Traits

The nine person is a seeker of knowledge. They will give away their last dime to the needy while on their quest. They are self sacrificing, and their desire to benefit from their knowledge and experience is strong. They are always ready to teach or give selflessly. To be selfless is the beginning process of learning universal love, understanding and compassion. If these lessons are not learned, then loss, sacrifice, loneliness, unhappiness, bad nerves and failure may result.

Greatness and success in all matters is their destiny. If it is true that the number one gets the world, it is likewise true that the number nine gets the universe. The nine wants the best of all possible worlds and will work hard to achieve it. They will never stop searching and their entire life is one endless exploration. They see possibility where other numbers see limitation. They have a special genius for seeing splendid things that the common mind might consider silly.

The nine wants to soar in life, and after landing remain unimpeded from all obstacles in life. However, this can cause some unsettling problems in their daily life, for no one can remain entirely free from strings. The nine wants life to be perfect. They don't want to waste their time with petty, moronic details or be bothered by a narrow- minded boss with no vision. In working with others, they have no compassion for a mediocre mentality. They are not tolerant of people they feel "not up to speed" with them. They are ruled by the planet Neptune and are devoted to philosophy and the belief that higher learning, mystic and super-natural forces can guide their every step.

A classic trait of the nine is their fighting disposition; sometimes arguing just for the sake of argument! They will start life "swimming upstream against the tide" and largely due to their perseverance they will almost always prevail in the end. The fearless and brave characteristics of the nine are to be envied. No one can make the nine feel slighted, for their opinion of them-selves is backed by strong convictions.

The nine can come across as being rash, rude and impulsive, and appear to actually not care what others think of them. The nine feels the need to be in control of their environment. If not, they often strive to rule their own fate. This necessary control factor will frustrate them frequently, as no one can ever completely change what the future has to hold for them. They must also try to control their impatience and temper, as this will only hinder them in all their goals. Their commanding nature and organizational abilities are positive aspects of their personality, and they need to harness them. Those aspects are gifts which should be used often in their life.

Careers

Prudent choices for careers would be medicine, social work, law, the arts, public relations or even theater. Acting is a marvelous way for them to project their sensitive views on many issues to a wide range of people. Their greatest success could lie in these fields. They must learn to follow their heart, for it is the single greatest barometer the nine possesses, and will never lead them astray.

Relationships

Aggression, vigor and strength are their hallmarks. They come to the surface in both their romantic and sentimental sides. Making love can be a show of great intensity, force and stamina. However, for all this, the number nine can be readily dominated when in love. The feeling of supremacy and control in love and passionate affairs is of paramount importance to the number nine person. So long as they can keep in check their tendency to be temperamental and rash in both their words and deeds, their relationships should not suffer.

The greatest force in the life of the nine person is love. Love in all its forms: love of self, love of spouse, love of child, and love of a higher spirit are most important to them. They know how to cultivate each of these loves without compromising on any of the others. Such is their prowess in this area. Their ability to give as well as receive love is equally vital. They cannot function if they are always on the giving end of a relationship, nor are they happy to always be on the receiving end. They look for balance to be maintained.

So sensitive is the number nine to those around them, that they will hurt when others are hurt, and be elated when others are happy. They can give without "strings attached", for it is the act of giving to others that truly pleases them. Fortunately, they aren't usually accused of being self centered or solitary. They feel they belong to the world and world belongs to them. The nine must learn to remain neutral in life, otherwise others will often be hurt by their simply taking sides in a situation. The nine may forfeit friendships, money or even social standing should they do this too often.

The number nine is assigned to the planet Mars, and the second day of the week, Monday, is their best day. Those born in the months of March, April, August, November and December are most compatible with the nine, as well as those whose birth dates add up to the numbers 1, 3, 6 and 9. Those born in the months of January, May, July and October may cause real, not imagined, problems for the number nine. The same is true for those whose birth dates add up to the numbers 2, 7 and 8.

18/9

1: Independence and Confidence

8: Abundance and Power

9: Honesty and Wisdom

Color: *Rose, Red Pink*

Gem: *Diamond*

Crystal: *Pyrite*

Planet: *The Sun*

Day of the Week: *Thursday*

Much of their inner strength comes from the giving to others from their own heart and mind. There is no need to show them how to give, for they can do it on their own, for it is innate. In other words, when they hear opinions of others, they rather take from their own intuitions. It should be emphasized that it is of utmost importance to feel it necessary to follow their own convictions. When working, they are naturally independent humanitarians that possess leadership qualities as well as executive and administrative capabilities. Although their talents don't always blossom early in life, such talents do eventually come forward.

If they ever learn to use such talents in serving others (meaning all mankind in general), they will find the potential for accomplishment and financial reward through their work. For everything they tend to do, whether in business or in a relationship, they tend to have very strong personal needs and desires; which all stem from their nature of feeling that they need some power. 18/9 people tend to be a little self-centered, and desire to have an abundance of money to satisfy their material needs.

Shy they are not, but more the aggressive, ambitious and self-confident type. Ready and able to work on a task, they are efficient and dependable. They make themselves very aware of their surroundings, and you can trust that when given an assignment, they will make things happen in an organized fashion.

If they are not working to the best of their ability they can be very introverted, rigid, and stubborn, losing touch with their higher spirit and their own spiritual essence. They can be opinionated and always believe that there is fault in the world, becoming upset with its lack of perfection. When they get angry or upset, they try to deal with the situation on a spiritual level.

In relationships, they truly go out of their way to show an interest in their partner. They usually get along with partners that are willing to work with them, and they usually get along with friends of their partners as well. They are indeed social and always look for honesty in their mate. Honesty is an issue with them, and without a strong sense of it, their relationship can become difficult.

If they haven't already chosen an intelligent companion, they will not stay in the relationship unless their companion is continually improving themselves. Even if their partner is not perfect (although perfection is something they look for in their mate), they need to know that "the elevator goes all the way to the top."

The 18/9 individuals are Romantic, but not so much in a heart-felt manner. Romance to them can be the provision of material things if they have the money to provide them. They are good judges of character, so they are pretty good at guessing what their mate may want. Love for the 18/9 tends to come from the mental state and they are not hurt as easily as other nine persons. However, they do express love and affection outwardly , and will do everything they can for you without asking for much in return.

27/9

2: Cooperation

7: Trust and Openness

9: Honesty and Wisdom

Color: *Rose, Red Pink*

Gem: *Diamond*

Crystal: *Pyrite*

Planet: *The Sun*

Day of the Week: *Thursday*

True to life and loving individuals, they work best when around other people. Hard workers, they like challenges, and are creative and analytical in nature. When they believe in something and believe that others should do it the way they suggest, they don't just tell them, they show by example.

Many people consider them different from the norm whenever they approach an assignment and finally come up with a solution. Their solution usually is more the alternative answer than the one expected by others. This is why it is hard for people to understand them. While people are busy trying to figure them out, they are busy doing the same thing. Usually, they are trying to understand the next person and why they came up with the conclusion they did. In other words, they just don't portray any easy perceptions of themselves or others.

If not careful, they would not be fun to be with when they obtain negative vibes. They can become extremely sensitive and irrational, and makes it difficult to give or even receive affection from others. They lose sense in following their own intuition, which is in fact their true guiding light. The 27/9 can experience constant swing moods of depression, unfriendliness and uncaring thoughts. At times, they may also give too much in the way of friendship, only to get stepped on.

In relationships, it will take some time before they actually become comfortable in giving of themselves. When they do, they are quick to believe they understand their mate and quick to provide a helping hand to their partner, or to those that their partner cares about. At times, they will definitely appear aloof or cold, but this is just a protective shield until they can trust you as their soul companion. Once trust is embedded, then they will open up the world to the person they are involved with.

Caution as to what is said to them. The 27/9 is an oversensitive individual and thinks directly from the heart. If giving them personal criticism, they will not take it well. They will spend a great deal of their time analyzing what was said about them as opposed to doing something more productive.

As much as they love to help out others, they are by no means a doormat. They can be quite conservative and concentrate on themselves just the same. They may or may not always be confident in what they do, but when working a positive energy, they will always depend upon themselves.

Always lending a shoulder to cry on, they provide a sympathetic and tolerant ear. They pay close attention to what is being said about them or others. Without much convincing, they do not hide the fact that they are idealistic and at times creative and practical.

Social and diplomatic in their approach to situations, they are never far from people who admire them. They can compromise their way into and out of a situation, making it easy for a person to find them practical enough to become involved with them. They can go anywhere and be accepted. This gives the hint that they would love taking romantic walks in the park, holding hands, and giving massages. They enjoy making the person they are around feel warm and appreciated, looking for admiration in return.

36/9

3: Expression and Sensitivity

6: Balance, Responsibility, Vision and Love

9: Honesty and Wisdom

Color: *Rose, Red Pink*

Gem: *Diamond*

Crystal: *Pyrite*

Planet: *The Sun*

Day of the Week: *Thursday*

If anyone were to ask where they can find a person that can lend a helping hand, look no further, for the 36/9 is always ready, able and willing to help out their fellow man or woman. Sympathetic and kind, they neglect the drive of being self-centered, which in turn actually helps themselves to be more generous with personal and material resources of others. If their dealings with other individuals happens to lead them into compromising situations, there is no need to worry, for they are capable of rectifying any situation with a delicate balance that anyone would envy.

If they are working against the laws of the spirit, their energy becomes scattered; losing focus on whatever it is they are doing. Their emotional level becomes very high and blocks their rational thoughts. They begin to lack affection, tell many lies, and become too involved in trivial and superficial matters. Their temper is usually short and possesses them with a sharp tongue to lash out with many verbal assaults.

For a person seeking a full fledged relationship that carries the whole nine yards, this individual focuses much of their time on having or maintaining a family. They show tremendous love for children, and children love to be around them, especially if they happen to be a teacher. If children or adults are to learn from them, they usually don't learn from them giving opinions as to what to do, but they show them by giving an example that should be followed.

It would be wise to be careful in expressing what one feels to this type of person. They can be extremely emotional, and feel hurt very quickly. So quickly, that their short temper can flare to a crescendo, pushing their mate away from them; no longer wanting to be involved.

They thrive on honesty, and even more so when trying to deal with the issue of dealing with honesty within themselves.

Affection and touch is something they cherish. They tend to heal through the power of their hands and eventually look for the reciprocal effect from people they care about. Not always looking for something in return, but always doing for others, they do it unlike anyone else, and deserve to be appreciated.

A walk on the beach, a picnic in a secluded spot, or taking them ballroom dancing makes their artistic feelings come to life and show their partner that they really enjoy their company. Whatever activity, it must be creative or have some creative touch to keep them interested in the relationship.

They usually show tremendous interest in being with and around others. These are humanitarian oriented people and they will do their best with their talents when given the opportunity. Consider them the type of individuals that are very social, crowd pleasing, and the type of person that can sell you a car or outright just entertain those they come in contact with. Talking or writing is a natural gift, and it makes them feel great whenever they are able to help others through what was said or written.

45/9

4: Practicality and Stability
5: Freedom and Discipline
9: Honesty and Wisdom

Color: *Rose, Red Pink*

Gem: *Diamond*

Crystal: *Pyrite*

Planet: *The Sun*

Day of the Week: *Thursday*

Consider them admired philanthropists who are practical, idealistic and hard working in the benefit of others. When people need help, they don't have a problem volunteering, as long they don't feel as if they are about to be used. They undoubtedly work well with others, and when working on a project, they are methodical and systematic in their approach. Always able to think through a project or situation, they are no doubt rational people. No matter what the scenario, they tend to take any situation and effectively analyze it in front of you or in private. Overall, they are able to take on any situation and create stability.

These people thrive on something new, different and challenging. This is what helps them to help themselves and others go to a higher spiritual level of improving themselves, their situation or task. These quick and clever thinkers have a great ability to analyze the moment, situation or project and work upon it with grace and style. If they are to help, expect them to come up with ways that makes things easier for them or others to complete the task. Their ingenuity is so sharp that it helps them to come up with ideas that help them from becoming bored with a monotonous or routine task.

If however, they choose not to trust and not to listen to their own intuition or inner spirit, then expect that anything they do will go wrong. Then, when they make an analysis of a situation, it may appear irrational, disorganized and confusing. Their goals may seem set, but they remain stagnant in reaching them. No longer will they feel or be dependable around others, and their lack of organization and impatience will keep them at bay. Their rigid and stubborn views will in fact make it hard for them to see the whole picture in a relationship, which makes it even harder for commitment to play a role in the relationship.

45/9s are delightful people to spend time with in a relationship. Outgoing and looking to travel off to far away places, they remain practical. Truly seekers of love, they will do anything for their partner if they feel spiritually fulfilled, and will not ask for anything in return, at least not right away. They believe that helping themselves and others helps them control whatever task comes about in their relationship. This is what they believe is the true way that they can make practical advancements in relationships. They are great family makers and are very capable of building a strong home. Given the opportunity, they are very supportive in all that their partner does.

Notes & Calculations

Notes & Experiences

Master Numbers

These Numbers Represent Special Gifts and Should Not be Reduced to a Single Digit. If a person has not appeared to harness the special gifts granted them by the Creator, then they may have their number reduced to a single digit.

11

The
Enlightened
One

Destiny Number
29/11/ 2

Master 11

11: Double Independence and Confidence

9: Honesty and Wisdom

2: Cooperation

Color: *Orange*

Gem: *Moonstone*

Crystal: *Rutile*

Planet: *Moon*

Day of the Week: *Monday*

Here is a person that represents the essence of extreme powers, confidence and independence. This number two person, derived from the principles of the Master 11, are among the few that work their energies from a higher order; as do others that also possess a master number. With their talents, they are among the highest of achievers and can usually obtain some of the highest recognition throughout their walk in life.

When focused, anything they wish to master comes easier, and they stand out in the crowd because of their great vigor, vitality and endurance. Many people may notice their aimless ways of approaching different things, and continually advise them to either focus or stick to one thing or the other. Although it is their nature to be that way.

Spiritual in nature, they possess a great ability to inspire others, and are usually at their best when they help others achieve. A person with such a master number does in fact have a special energy, but negatively they are apt to display a sense of insecurity either in public or among their own thoughts.

Whenever this person enters a room, they command the platform. When the platform is given to them, whether it is one person or a mass of people, they can help move them in any direction, helping them achieve an objective. If any particular type of person can, they are among the top in making a difference for others. Many times, they find themselves doing for others rather than solely for themselves. Working in cooperation with other people is their natural forte.

However, placing them on tight schedules and giving them strict orders is not how they like to operate, for it makes them very uncomfortable—uncomfortable to the point that they tend to procrastinate. They are at their best when they feel free in helping others or working at a pace they deem comfortable.

Caution. So emotional is the 29/11/2 that it haunts them frequently. If this person doesn't get things their way, they tend to express themselves in a competitive manner since they fear losing or feeling insecure. If they are just too small or perhaps unable to compete at the moment, they become determined to become someone of big importance. Not only to be big before the person or group of persons that made them feel threatened initially, but for the world to see. Proving superiority is a constant thought on their mind. They believe that they can do almost anything, if not master anything, given the opportunity coupled with their own personal desire.

This master 29/11/2 person has tendencies to be strongly opinionated, and they are skillful at imposing their views upon others in an intimidating or bossy manner. If you wish to change their opinion, you can do so. However, prepare for a friendly but intense verbal debate. Only the dominant one shall prevail!

They may appear stubborn and unwilling to change since they have a hard time letting go, especially in relationships. In time they soften up due to their emotional nature. If they do not change, they sometimes find themselves trying to control their extra energy in behaviors of abuse or addiction to unhealthy substances. The judicial system will usually find its way into their lives if they cannot control themselves.

With such charisma and charm, their personality makes them very attractive and exciting to be with. When all energies in their strong magnetic and stimulating fields are clear, expect the best from them, for they will give you nothing less. However, if their energy is blocked, expect their insecurity characteristics to surface. This characteristic may eventually lead to a difficult relationship.

The 29/11/2 is the sentimental companion that inhibits their own emotional expression, since they tend to concentrate on the creative energies in their own mind. Their sensitivity is so strong that they try very hard to mentally control their own situations, causing this person to withhold or logically rationalize their feelings. They tend to avoid expressing hurt feelings, and may even appear cold and uncaring. All of these inhibitions are due to the lack of an emotional appearance or "shield" used to protect themselves. These shields can play a major role in affecting their interpersonal relationships.

The 29/11/2 definitely looks for relationships as do other numbers, and values them highly since they tend to have a hard time understanding themselves. They have unique ways about themselves, unlike any other number, and this is mainly due to the master number involved in their makeup. Here is an Illuminati, (The Enlightened One) when their talents have been tapped.

Very rarely do you find them without many friends or contacts. However, due to their sensitive nature, they are and should be careful in selecting their friends and contacts. This is especially true when placing their confidence in others. They will find that they look for support from others, and this is the basis upon which many of their relationships are created. For the 29/11/2, relationships can become difficult at times since their double one energy continually pulls them towards seeking independence from people and things.

The 29/11/2 contains a strong magnetic energy field. So much so, that they can become attractive to many people as far as popularity, loving relationships and personality are concerned. If their energies happen to be blocked in any manner, then repression of emotion, feelings of insecurity, and over sensitivity will result. Relationships will then surely suffer. To emphasize again, their energy is so strong that if they are involved in a project they enjoy, or see as a necessity, they will bury themselves in it. This overall makes them too busy to participate in a loving relationship, but they fare well in business relationships.

With the 29/11/2, you will never have to worry if they get along with people. It is their magnetism, charisma and positive creative energy that makes them the renaissance individualists. No matter what they choose to do, their spiritual and mental plane runs high, helping them along until the project is finished. They do not have to be the life of the party, but find their best energies used when they network with other people.

Just as they attract people, you will find that they attract money in the same fashion. Their energy is not only high, but when positive, money is just another form of energy that they attract. With their energy channeled properly, expect to see them become extremely wealthy, a solution to some of their inhibitions or insecurities. This is not to say all of them. For if their energy is not positive, they will find themselves without money and possibly in huge debt for a long period of time. At least until they get themselves together again.

Being tied down to a commitment is not easy for the 29/11/2 to handle. Remember, they have a scattered energy and when they are involved in what they believe is an important project, the relationship will take a back seat. Their minds are always flowing with creativity and they will look to maintain a sense of independence, forfeiting a relationship or putting it to the side until the project is complete. Even though they have many friends and contacts they have a sentimental side to them, and seek more associates and valued companions in relationships.

These individuals lead an exciting life with an enormous amount of energy to keep pace in any activity they choose to tackle. Since their energy always appears to run so high, when they show signs of being weary, they may have had their energy level collapse. Rest is in order, and they will be back on the go once rest is taken.

Destiny Number
38/11/ 2

Master 11

11: Double Independence and Confidence

3: Expression and Sensitivity

8: Abundance and Power

2: Cooperation

Color: *Orange*

Gem: *Moonstone*

Crystal: *Rutile*

Planet: *Moon*

Day of the Week: *Monday*

Looking for a bright, independently creative leader or advisor? Well you have found a person with such chemistry. This is the type of person that you can find moving masses of people with their creativity. They do this in most of the tasks they take on, whether it is leading a team, a country or convincing you to buy a product on their infomercial. The 38/11/2 always shines bright. If they need money, they can usually attract it to themselves. However, they are much better at attracting people with their positive energy.

Money tends to automatically follow them. Not so much in abundance, but enough for them to acknowledge that money is not always one of their top worries. Given the opportunity, expect a person that would be quite efficient in all that they set out to do. If making money is involved, they handle the opportunity very well -- so much so, that it is something to be admired. Not all of these individuals wish to have material satisfaction, or constantly concentrate on it. It is the control over the masses, large or small, that they usually prefer.

Emotionally, they tend to express little either in business or personal relationships because they are so emotionally rigid. This rigidity can make it very difficult for a partner or loved one to feel a part of them. It is not intentional, they just have a very difficult time expressing themselves. When they do begin to express themselves, look out. They may say what you think is the wrong thing in an effort to express themselves the best way they know how.

Independent and cooperative are these individuals, whereby helping other people with their talents can open doors to help others achieve their goals. People usually have a strong mental or physical attraction to the 38/11/2 energy. Such attraction is so strong, that if used in an abusive way, they will possibly end up becoming controlling, bossy, manipulative and constantly seeking power for all the wrong reasons. Money still can become a part of them because of their strong energy attraction, but the money will be obtained in an ill-fated fashion. If their energy field is depleted, expect possible abuse of alcohol, sex and drugs to become a factor in their lives.

When the positive energy is flowing, you have encountered a progressive and ambitiously determined individual. This is a person of strong will power and self confidence. Consider them a friendly, open and sociable character. Even though they are affectionate and loving, they prefer to have control of a situation or relationship. Give them a large project and they can handle it with no problem, for they are creative problem solvers. With such control issues, they usually get what they wish. However, if things do not go their way, they quickly move away from the situation.

Destiny Number 47/11/2

Master II

11: Double Independence and Confidence

4: Stability and Process

7: Trust and Openness

2: Cooperation and Balance

Color: *Orange*

Gem: *Moonstone*

Crystal: *Rutile*

Planet: *Moon*

Day of the Week: *Monday*

This is the character that will take what they have and entrust you with it. With this trust and openness, they are practical and reliable. They have good common sense and a great spiritual nature, a solid citizen and a very hard worker. There is nothing that they cannot learn, for they not only take in everything that is presented to them, but also, they are deep thinkers. Although analytical in thought, they tend to let their spirit guide them when it is time to make decisions; giving them a higher feeling of authority on the subject. When it comes to manual labor, they can take it or leave it.

Remember, this is a Master 11 person and they will no doubt attract money because of the energy that they possess. Their energy level is high because they have a master number and money is another energy that can be harnessed once the high level is achieved. Even though money is not a constant motivating factor in their lives, it comes to them without them going out of their way to always attain it.

The feeling of being very sensitive or being betrayed by someone they trust is always a great factor in their lives. This person tends to analyze anything and everything that is said to them, and this does not help them rectify their over sensitivity. They tend to shy away from people even if a crowd is surrounding them, unless they have finally come around and started to learn how to express themselves and work well with others. Until this is learned, they tend to live in their own shell instead of moving masses of people.

If they work with negative energy, they will experience confusion, lack of commitment and discipline, and a sense of disorder. All of these combined negative energies can develop into laziness and short-sightedness in their spiritual nature. The 47/11/2 is very prone to addiction of drugs, alcohol and tobacco if not careful. If positive energies are not expressed, they will continue to live in a world that tends to be imaginary, struggling to deal with reality as opposed to keeping their heads in the clouds .

Once this person can get past the issue of trusting their partner, then stability will clearly enter the picture. These are the type of people that will find it in their nature to form a partnership, or settle down into a marriage and have children. Anything that they take part in, work or family, you will find that they do it with independence, discipline and order. They tend to work hard at making a stable family. However, they continually need things to work on and be spiritually involved.

Notes & Calculations

Notes & Experiences

_____

_____

_____

_____

_____

_____

_____

_____

_____

_____

_____

_____

_____

_____

_____

_____

_____

_____

_____

_____

_____

_____

_____

_____

22

The
Master
Builder

Destiny Number 22/4

Master 22

4: Stability and Practicality

2: Cooperation and Balance

2: Cooperation and Balance

Color: *Green*

Gem: *Emerald, Green Jade*

Crystal: *Tinstone*

Planet: *Saturn*

Day of the Week: *Thursday*

Behold the Master Builder. This is the visionary who is the ultimate idealist that can make things happen on a large scale. No other number possesses such powerful traits for building and carrying out great plans to achieve goals. This is the recognized internationalist who contains the power to bring rank and order to the world. Their power can be so strong that it would be best used for helping humanity and not self gain. Their service of humanity is always rewarded by the creator.

Very practical is the basic description of their nature. Give them an assignment, and you can be sure that they will complete the job in the most thorough, efficient and insightful manner. More than any other type of person doing the same type of work. When encountering these people, you will find that they are very rational, exceptionally well organized, and systematic in all jobs they approach. Consider them the hardest worker of hard working individuals. They tend to take any situation and analyze it to the greatest extent, but overall they are able to take on the situation and create stability. Once this power is achieved, limitations upon this person will cease to exist.

If however, their energies are not in sync in a positive manner, then expect that their analysis of things become irrational, disorganized and confusing. Relationships will suffer because of their instability, and it will make the relationship unstable. Their rigid and stubborn views will in fact make it hard for them to see the whole picture in a relationship and much harder for them to stay committed to a relationship.

As service oriented persons, they would do well in business, if they are not already in business. Working hard and using their analytical skills is a tremendous asset for the 22/4 person. Although their energies do not attract money, their willingness to work hard helps them hold and organize their finances in a very efficient manner.

Relationships with these individuals are dynamic. Their energy and vibrations is uplifting, and those involved with them can see and feel these powerful vibrations. As long as a goal is spelled out for them, consider the goal achieved, and achieved in a very noticeable way. They work very hard in a relationship once they have accepted commitment which is difficult for the 22/4 because of their many and varied interests. Tying them down will be quite a challenge, even if you happen to be married to a 22/4. You see, as long as they feel that they can control whatever task comes about in their relationship, they can make practical advancements towards the relationship, and will do well. They are great family makers and are very capable of building a strong home.

When they finally do come around to accept commitment, they will work well with their partner, pay attention to their concerns, and be sensitive to their needs. They will work towards improving the relationship by executing any actions, starting with the smallest detail, at least until the big picture can be seen. Be careful in the handling of them, for they are very emotional, and oversensitive to personal criticism. They love to share and work well in duo activities with their spouse or partner, but have a difficult time expressing themselves. Therefore, the relationship can suffer and lead to a divorce because things that were bothering them for the longest were never discussed until it is practically too late, or the papers are already signed.

Notes & Calculations

_____

_____

_____

_____

_____

_____

_____

_____

_____

_____

_____

_____

_____

_____

_____

_____

_____

_____

_____

_____

_____

_____

_____

Notes & Experiences

228

The
Expressive
Communicators

Destiny Number 33/6

Master 33

3: Expression and Sensitivity

3: Expression and Sensitivity

6: Balance, Responsibility, Vision and Love

Color: Blue

Gem: Blue Sapphire, Blue White Pearl, Diamond

Crystal: Indicolite

Planet: Jupiter

Day of the Week: Sunday, Monday, Friday

Very warm and social, the home and hearth are usually of utmost importance, especially if they have children involved. The 33/6 possesses the powerful energy of the double three, a very difficult energy to harness. Only few have been able to bring this master number's true energy to life and make a difference in the world in which we all live.

The 33/6 cultivates friends and relations the way others cultivate their gardens: with tender loving care. Relationships are usually strongly bonded and they are more selective in who they actually consider their friends. When those that are dearest to them are around, and they feel their love and appreciation are threatened, they become defensive; almost to the point that violence is initiated. This is especially true in the case of children; definitely where protection of health and safety is concerned. Their true nature is their strong desire not to see family and close friends hurt.

Very service oriented, the 33/6 can accomplish tremendous things within their surrounding community or the world as a whole; not necessarily as a leader, but as an integral member of a great movement. They are true visionaries and see more in the way of massive achievement than any other number.

Some of their more negative aspects include, being prone to worry a great deal, becoming overly inflexible and combative if someone differs with their opinion. This may cause insecurity and they will feel the need for a lot of encouragement and praise to know their own worth. Once they fall out of the habit of doing things a particular way, they believed was effective for them but was not, things will become better for them. In the meantime, when their routine is disrupted, high emotions tend to take over, they become very sensitive and find it difficult to express themselves. They must try developing their self-esteem, and then they will find that they do not need the approval of others to measure their qualities.

Changing their mind is not easy, for they take a lot of convincing. They can debate with the best, since they believe everything has more than one side to an issue. They truly understand that there are three sides to every issue: his side, her side and the truth! They love to debate, sometimes just for the "sport" of the argument, not to alienate people. When the debate is over and the smoke clears, they make sure both sides walk away friends and not enemies. That is one of their greatest attributes, because others will go to them, giving them acceptance when later, they are in need of a thoughtful and patient sounding board for their troubles.

In relationships, the 33/6 individuals like routine and are creatures of habit. This is why domesticity and the trappings of home life are attractive to them. Running a smooth house-hold is almost second nature to them, and what a beautiful household it would be! Careful what is said to these individuals, for they a can be extremely emotional and sensitive if not shown extra love and appreciation, tenderness and attention. If they learn to keep such emotions under control, they can be very fun to spend time with.

They surely will bring a smile to your face and require little from you in a material sense, but would not mind having comfortable, if not luxurious surroundings. They know how to keep doing things their way as long as they remain happy. It is the finer things in life that appeal to the 33/6 personality, and they sur-round themselves with such. Since they are careful and prudent in money matters, don't worry, their investments will be solid, depend-able and steady. No wild market speculations for the six personality.

Notes & Calculations

Notes & Experiences

44

The
True
Stabilizers

Destiny Number 44/8

Master 44

4: Practicality and Stability

4: Practicality and Stability

Color: Rose, Red Pink

Gem: Diamond

Crystal: Pyrite

Planet: The Saturn

Day of the Week: Thursday

The special energy of this person can be one of admiration. Very, very practical is the basic description of their nature. These are the potential executives or managers that can do without administrators or corporate professional organizers to help them out. These individuals are so efficient that they can do it all by themselves. Particular and astute with details, they are not one to hesitate in accomplishing a task. They are ambitious and self-confident with a high working energy.

If an entire company must depend on them, they will always come through with flying colors. This is the double energy of a working number four, and by no means are they afraid of taking on an assignment; and when they do, have no problem tackling it. Their efficient nature gives them the good mind to plan ahead, organize, use a practical method and devise a system that is bound to work; following every detail to the end. Even if things may appear to be chaotic before they begin the project, trust in them and watch how they can reconstruct and build a strong foundation.

If however, their energies are not working in a positive manner, then expect any assessment of a situation they make to be irrational, disorganized and confusing. Even relationships will suffer because they can become unstable, stressed, doubtful and insecure, due to the feeling of a lack of authority in what they are good at doing. Their rigid and stubborn views will in fact make it hard for them to see the whole picture in a relationship, and then make it even harder for commitment to play a role in a relationship.

To experience and enjoy the most of their wonderful talents, they would be at their best if they were service oriented individuals.

Then they would find that people will follow their direction and respect their power and authority. Things work for them mostly through their overwhelming determination, perseverance, self-discipline and concentration. Usually then, and only then, will they amass a fortune, if fortune is what they are seeking. Remember even more so, that if they would concentrate on others instead of themselves, their fortune will come.

As long as the Master 44 person feels that they can control whatever task comes about in their relationship, and that they can make practical advancements, then they will do well. They are great family makers and providers, and are very capable of building a strong home.

In relationships, they are not into fooling themselves with unrealistic dreams, goals or fantasies. Whether they are in business or trying to find a mate, they are usually a good judge of character as to a person's credential or personality. Issues in their relationships however, tend to circle around control. That is, control of direction they wish to go and navigating direction of the relationship they are involved in. Only when in the driver's seat do they feel at their best to create stability in all they do, and make sure their family and companion is strongly supported and rooted with security.

Unless time and patience is spent with them, they will usually show little affection toward their mate. They need to be shown much love and appreciation for all the things that they do. Otherwise, they will not be committed for long, and feel bored because of their insecurity of feeling unrecognized. Their relationships, unlike others, usually come from left field and they think rationally before entering into one: helping them to approach another person by being very gentle instead of rigid.

Notes & Calculations

_____

_____

_____

_____

_____

_____

_____

_____

_____

_____

_____

_____

_____

_____

_____

_____

_____

_____

_____

_____

_____

_____

_____

_____

_____

_____

_____

Notes & Experiences

About The Authors

BERNARD A. ADOLPHUS

Internationally known, Bernard is one of the most recoginized numerologists in the world. With more than seventeen years of experience in his craft, he has helped people in all walks of life; especially the youth in churches and correctional facilities. Consultant, teacher, radio talk show co-host and analyst, Bernard travels the world educating people in the science of numerology.

Born in Belize, Central America and a graduate of Westley Public School, Bernard finds no task too great to accomplish when it comes to writing about numerology.

Requests for personal numerology readings have been overwhelming since the first printing of this book. New books authored by Bernard will be published soon.

DAVID E. SMITH JR.

Author and publisher of three books, David has broken new ground for his publishing company Destech Press Inc. (DES Technologies, Inc.), located in Peekskill, NY. In this book, David has provided the reader with valuable information that comes from more than nine years of study in the science of numerology. Not only does he write about numerology, but about various topics he finds interesting and beneficial to his readers.

In his first book called *Dreams and Numbers, Numbers and Dreams*, David gives the readers definitions of their dreams and lottery numbers associated with the defined dreams.

His third book, *Y2 Care about Issues and Events in the New Millennium; The Destruction of the U.S. Constitution and Our National*

Sovereignty Vol. I, David educates the reader about the Millennium Bug; the plan for a "One World Government;" protecting your wealth in gold and silver coinage; and survival skills.

David has been writing extensively since his college years at SUNY Oswego, in Oswego, NY; SUNY Buffalo Law School in Buffalo, NY; and while an Assistant District Attorney in White Plains, NY. Seminars, audio tapes, a talk radio show and newsletters have given David recognition in the literary field, whereby he now consults on various topics. It is the love for the art of writing that keeps him going.